Greatness

AWAITS YOU

Greatness
AWAITS YOU

DR. NORA SHARIFF-BORDEN

Contents

A Note from the Author

Thank you for purchasing this book—*Greatness Awaits You*. It is not by accident that this book has found its way into your hands. I believe that within every individual lies a unique purpose, an untapped potential, and an extraordinary destiny waiting to unfold.

Each and every one of you has been created with greatness inside of you! You were not made for mediocrity; you were designed to accomplish the impossible. Your life is a testament to divine craftsmanship, a masterpiece in the making. God has placed within you the power, strength, and wisdom to become the very best version of yourself. No matter where you are in life, no matter what challenges you have faced, remember that you are destined for more. You are not defined by your past, your mistakes, or your struggles—your greatness is already within you, waiting to be discovered, nurtured, and unleashed.

Writing has always been more than just a passion for me— it is a calling. Through my words, I seek to uplift, inspire, and empower you. This book is my way of pouring into your journey, reminding you of the incredible potential you

"Decide today not to sit on your Greatness!"

possess. If even one sentence in these pages' sparks hope, fuels your ambition, or ignites a new perspective, then my purpose as an author has been fulfilled.

I encourage you to embrace this journey with an open heart and a willing spirit. As you turn each page, let these words serve as a reminder that you are more than capable, you are chosen, and you are destined for greatness.

May this book be a source of inspiration, strength, and transformation in your life. **Greatness Awaits you! Now is the time to step into it**

Blessings

Dr. Nora Shariff-Borden

"Decide today not to sit on your Greatness!"

"Greatness Awaits You!
There Is Nothing Impossible For You"

Acknowledgments

First and foremost, I give all glory and thanks to You, Lord, for filling my heart and mind with the words to write this powerful book, *Greatness Awaits You*. Thank You for revealing the incredible power You have placed within me—the power to walk in greatness in all that I do.

To my beloved mother, thank you for always believing in me and my visions. You were the epitome of greatness—strong, determined, and full of wisdom. You instilled in me the value of hard work and perseverance, and for that, I am forever grateful. I love and miss you deeply. How I wish you were here to witness the fruits of your unwavering love and support. Your guidance has shaped me into the successful businesswoman I am today. You raised four powerful, God-fearing daughters, and your legacy of faith and resilience lives on in us. You were truly one of a kind.

To my beautiful sisters, thank you for your unwavering love, encouragement, and support. Your presence in my life is a true blessing.

"Decide today not to sit on your Greatness!"

"Greatness Awaits You!
There Is Nothing Impossible For You"

To my incredible husband, your steadfast support in everything I do means the world to me. Thank you for always standing by my side. I love you beyond words.

To my wonderful children, my greatest desire as your mother is to lead by example, walking in faith and purpose. I am so proud of each of you. I thank God every day for choosing me to be your mother.

To my precious grandchildren, you are my inspiration. I love you with the love of Christ, and I pray that you always remember—through Him, *all things are possible.*

To my extraordinary and powerful pastor, the Reverend Dr. Cynthia Hale, thank you for being a beacon of strength and perseverance. You have shattered barriers and silenced doubters, proving that God qualifies those He calls. Your confidence in God's vision has been a profound lesson for me. Thank you for teaching us that with faith, dedication, and a willingness to pay the price for our dreams, *anything* is possible.

With a heart full of gratitude, I honor each of you who has played a part in my journey. May God bless you abundantly.

"Decide today not to sit on your Greatness!"

Preface

Greatness Awaits You is more than just a book—it is a call to action, a divine affirmation, and a guide to unlocking the potential that resides within you. It serves as a reminder that God has placed within each of us the seeds of greatness, waiting to be nurtured and developed. Too often, life's challenges, past failures, and personal doubts cause us to forget or underestimate the immense purpose that has been instilled in us by our Creator. This book is designed to awaken, strengthen, and propel you toward the life of greatness that God has destined for you.

Throughout the pages of this book, you will discover that greatness is not reserved for a select few; it is a gift, an inherent part of who you are. God's plan has always been to shape, mold, and guide you into becoming the best version of yourself—a person of impact, influence, and purpose. This journey requires faith, perseverance, and an unshakable belief in God's promises. The truth is, the greatness within you is not defined by the world's standards of success, but by your willingness to walk in obedience to God's calling.

"Decide today not to sit on your Greatness!"

"Greatness Awaits You!
There Is Nothing Impossible For You"

As you embark on this journey, I encourage you to open your heart, clear your mind of doubts, and embrace the reality that you are chosen for something extraordinary. This book will not only inspire but will also provide you with practical steps, scriptural insights, and real-life testimonies that confirm God's unwavering desire for you to live a life of significance.

You are not here by accident. Your dreams, talents, and passions were divinely placed within you for a reason. Greatness is already inside you—waiting to be activated, developed, and unleashed. My prayer is that this book will serve as a transformational tool in your life, helping you to see yourself through the lens of God's divine plan.

So, take this journey with an open heart, knowing that **Greatness Awaits You**. The time to step into your calling is now. Let this book be the confirmation and catalyst that propels you toward the incredible purpose that God has prepared for you.

"Decide today not to sit on your Greatness!"

Dr. Nora Shariff-Borden

Dr. Nora Shariff-Borden and her three younger sisters were born and raised in Boston, Massachusetts. She and her husband, Neil, live outside Atlanta, Georgia, and together they have six adult children, 14 grandchildren, and four great-grandchildren.

The seed of Christianity was planted in her life by her Grandmother, Nora Dunn. Dr. Nora moved away from the Lord and became a Muslim, but she woke up and realized an emptiness that was in her spirit, and that she missed her Lord and Savior, Jesus Christ. God saw fit to bring her back to Him over 30 years ago, and she accepted her call from God to become a Christian inspirational speaker.

In 2019, Dr. Nora founded Business Women On The Move For God (BWOTMFG). This organization inspires and encourages people to be who God has called them to be, which is awesome, powerful, mighty, and great. God wants them to be clear about their goals and dreams and how to achieve them through Him. She started BWOTMFG because she loves seeing people own their greatness and learn how to walk in it daily! She wants the next generation

"Decide today not to sit on your Greatness!"

of young people to realize their greatness and be unapologetic about it. Dr. Nora wants people to be able to get up when they have fallen and to learn the importance of continuing their journey! She wants them to be bold about their relationship with their Lord Jesus Christ.

Dr. Nora is also the Founder and CEO of Spiritual Touch TV, where she hosts a weekly online show, Real Conversations With Nora, which focuses on the many issues that people face every day through transparent conversations. She digs deep to help people talk about their issues to help them reclaim their authentic selves and overcome their obstacles so they can navigate through life successfully. Most importantly, the interviewees have a good time!

Dr. Nora believes she has a gift from God that allows her to connect with God's people. She believes that when you touch the heart of people, they will do all they can to support you. Her goal is to teach people that their words have the power to change their lives. She also believes she can help them paint a picture of what they want their life to look like so that when it appears, all they have to do is step into it.

She is a woman with a serious mission who believes that if she meets true needs of God's people with total sincerity

"Decide today not to sit on your Greatness!"

and commitment to serve as God has called her to do, her work will not be in vain.

Dr. Nora is the visionary of Powerful Women United Worldwide (PWUW). The mission of PWUW is to empower and support women of all backgrounds, ages, and walks of life to achieve their full potential. This group strives to create a safe and inclusive space where women can connect, learn, and grow together and where their unique voices and contributions are valued and celebrated.

In March of 2022, Dr. Nora was bestowed an Honorary Doctorate Degree from Trinity International University of Ambassadors (TIUA). On December 3rd of, 2022, she received the Presidential Lifetime Achievement Award. Also, in February of 2023, in honor of Black History Month, Dr. Nora was awarded The Presidential Legacy Lifetime Achievement Award from Trinity International University of Ambassadors in honor of our 44th President, Barack Obama.

In June of 2023, she was awarded The International Anthology of the Year Award by TIUA School of Business for Your Faith Will Make You Unstoppable.

On June 12th, 2024, She was presented with a resolution honoring her from Representative Billy Mitchell and

"Decide today not to sit on your Greatness!"

"Greatness Awaits You!
There Is Nothing Impossible For You"

Dr. Jacqueline Mohair, Founder of Trinity International University of Ambassadors at Georgia Capital! This honor was presented to her for being selected to serve as a United Nations Peace Ambassador to the United Nations in New York!

Her future project for BWOTMFG is to establish a $10,000 scholarship program for young women who major in business.

"Great things happen when people have Great Expectations!"

Stay in touch with Dr. Nora Shariff-Borden and Business Women On The Move For God by following us on.
Instagram @bwotmfg
Facebook @BusinessWomenontheMoveforGod
Facebook @ Spiritual Touch TV
YouTube @NoraShariff3505
You can also visit https://www.bwotmfg.com/.
Dr. Nora Shariff-Borden
Founder and CEO of BWOTMFG
info@bwotmfg.com
www.spiritualtouchtv.com

"Decide today not to sit on your Greatness!"

Chapter 1

"Growth is painful. Change is painful, but there is nothing more painful than staying stuck and not reaching your greatness."

"Decide today not to sit on your Greatness!"

"Greatness Awaits You!
There Is Nothing Impossible For You"

Life is a continuous journey of transformation, a path filled with challenges, struggles, and growth. While the thought of evolving into a better version of oneself is inspiring, the process of growth and change is often uncomfortable and even painful. However, what is far more agonizing than the pain of growth or change is the feeling of being stuck—remaining in a place of stagnation, watching time pass while knowing deep down that you are not living up to your full potential.

The Pain of Growth

Growth requires stepping outside of one's comfort zone, confronting fears, and embracing the unknown. It demands discipline, perseverance, and resilience. Whether it's personal, professional, emotional, or spiritual growth, the process often involves breaking old habits, adopting new mindsets, and pushing beyond perceived limits.

Just as muscles tear before they become stronger, personal growth involves shedding past limitations, outdated beliefs, and unhealthy attachments. It forces us to face our weaknesses and work through them. This process is rarely easy—it requires patience, effort, and endurance. But in the end, the rewards are undeniable: self-improvement, new opportunities, and a sense of fulfillment.

"Decide today not to sit on your Greatness!"

The Pain of Change

Change disrupts familiarity. It challenges the routines and patterns that feel safe and predictable. Whether it is transitioning to a new career, leaving a toxic relationship, moving to a different city, or adopting a healthier lifestyle, change often feels intimidating. It comes with uncertainty, and with uncertainty comes fear.

Many resist change because it forces them to abandon the security of what they know. But staying in the same place, refusing to embrace transformation, leads to complacency. And complacency, over time, turns into regret. While the pain of change is temporary, the regret of not changing can last a lifetime.

The Greater Pain of Being Stuck

The greatest suffering comes not from growth or change, but from standing still while knowing that you are capable of more. Staying stuck—whether in a dead-end job, a toxic environment, an unfulfilling relationship, or a negative mindset—leads to frustration, unhappiness, and a loss of purpose.

When people ignore their potential, they often experience feelings of dissatisfaction, restlessness, and regret. Watching others evolve while remaining stagnant can feel suffocating.

"Decide today not to sit on your Greatness!"

Over time, the realization that one has wasted years due to fear, doubt, or procrastination can be the most painful burden to bear.

Breaking Free and Reaching Greatness

Reaching one's full potential requires courage. It requires the willingness to endure temporary discomfort for long-term fulfillment. The key to overcoming stagnation is embracing growth and change, no matter how difficult.

Recognize the Fear but Move Forward Anyway – Fear is a natural response to the unknown, but it should not be a barrier. Acknowledge the fear, understand it, and push through it.

Adopt a Growth Mindset – Accept challenges as opportunities to learn rather than obstacles. Every setback is a lesson, every failure is a stepping stone.

Take Action, Even if Small – Progress happens through consistent action. Small steps toward change eventually lead to transformation.

Surround Yourself with Growth-Oriented People – Being around individuals who are striving for excellence will inspire and motivate you to do the same.

"Decide today not to sit on your Greatness!"

Trust the Process – Growth and change take time. Be patient and committed to the journey.

Conclusion: At the core of it all, the choice is clear: endure the temporary pain of growth and change or suffer the life-long pain of regret. True greatness lies on the other side of fear, and the only way to reach it is to embrace the discomfort that comes with transformation.

"Decide today not to sit on your Greatness!"

"Greatness Awaits You!
There Is Nothing Impossible For You"

"Decide today not to sit on your Greatness!"

"Greatness Awaits You!
There Is Nothing Impossible For You"

"Decide today not to sit on your Greatness!"

Chapter 2

"You don't have to have it all figured out to achieve your greatness!"

"Decide today not to sit on your Greatness!"

"Greatness Awaits You!
There Is Nothing Impossible For You"

Many people hesitate to pursue their dreams or take bold steps toward success because they feel unprepared, uncertain, or lacking in direction. However, the truth is that greatness is not achieved by having all the answers from the start—it is a journey of growth, learning, and perseverance.

Embracing the Journey Over Perfection

Success is not a straight path, and waiting until everything is perfectly aligned can hold you back from making meaningful progress. Life is full of uncertainties, and even the most accomplished individuals started with doubts, questions, and incomplete plans. What separates them from others is their willingness to take the first step despite not having everything figured out.

Learning Through Experience

Many of life's most valuable lessons are learned along the way. No amount of preparation can substitute for the wisdom gained through real-world experience. As you take action toward your goals, you will gain knowledge, develop skills, and refine your approach. The journey itself will shape you into the person you need to become.

"Decide today not to sit on your Greatness!"

Overcoming Fear and Doubt

Fear of failure and self-doubt are common barriers to success. However, waiting for the "perfect moment" often leads to missed opportunities. The key is to start where you are, with what you have, and trust that you will figure out the rest as you go. Confidence grows with each step forward, and even setbacks contribute to your personal and professional development.

Progress Over Perfection

Achieving greatness is about progress, not perfection. Small, consistent steps lead to significant achievements over time. Rather than focusing on having every detail figured out, focus on taking meaningful action, adjusting as needed, and embracing the process of continual improvement.

The Power of Adaptability

In an ever-changing world, the ability to adapt is crucial. New challenges, unexpected detours, and unforeseen opportunities will arise. Those who embrace flexibility and are willing to learn along the way are the ones who ultimately succeed. Greatness is not about knowing everything in advance but about being resilient and resourceful in the face of uncertainty.

"Decide today not to sit on your Greatness!"

"Greatness Awaits You!
There Is Nothing Impossible For You"

Trusting Yourself and Your Potential

Believing in yourself is essential. Even without a clear road-map, you have the ability to navigate challenges, find solu-tions, and grow into your full potential. Trust that your skills, passion, and determination will guide you forward, even if you don't have everything mapped out in advance.

Conclusion

The path to greatness is not about having all the answers—it's about having the courage to start. Every great achiever began somewhere, often with uncertainty and unanswered questions. What sets them apart is their willingness to take action, embrace growth, and persist despite challenges. So, take that first step today—because you don't have to have it all figured out to achieve your greatness!

"Decide today not to sit on your Greatness!"

"Greatness Awaits You!
There Is Nothing Impossible For You"

"Decide today not to sit on your Greatness!"

"Greatness Awaits You!
There Is Nothing Impossible For You"

"Decide today not to sit on your Greatness!"

Chapter 3

A Strong Woman Finds Her Strength in God and Won't Be Moved, No Matter What!

"Decide today not to sit on your Greatness!"

"Greatness Awaits You!
There Is Nothing Impossible For You"

A strong woman is not defined by her physical power, wealth, or the approval of others. Instead, her strength is deeply rooted in her unwavering faith in God. She stands firm, anchored in His promises, and remains unshaken by the trials and tribulations of life. No matter what challenges come her way—whether storms of uncertainty, heartbreak, setbacks, or adversity—her foundation in God makes her resilient, courageous, and steadfast.

Her Strength Comes from God

A strong woman recognizes that her strength does not come from her own abilities but from the One who created her. She draws her power from her relationship with God, relying on prayer, worship, and the wisdom of His Word. She understands that in her weakest moments, God's strength is made perfect (2 Corinthians 12:9). Instead of allowing fear or doubt to consume her, she leans on the divine assurance that God is her refuge, her fortress, and her ever-present help in times of trouble (Psalm 46:1).

Unshakable in the Face of Challenges

Life throws hardships at everyone, but a strong woman who trusts in God does not crumble under pressure. She may face disappointments, betrayal, financial struggles, or the loss of loved ones, but she remains rooted in faith. Her

"Decide today not to sit on your Greatness!"

hope is not in the world, but in the unchanging nature of God. Like a tree planted by the waters (Jeremiah 17:7-8), she does not wither when the heat of trials comes. Instead, she continues to flourish because she knows that God is working all things together for her good (Romans 8:28).

Firm in Her Identity and Purpose

A strong woman does not seek validation from society, relationships, or material possessions. She knows that she is fearfully and wonderfully made (Psalm 139:14) and that her worth comes from being a daughter of the Most High. She understands that God has given her a purpose, and she walks boldly in it, refusing to be swayed by negativity, doubt, or opposition. She does not allow her past mistakes or the opinions of others to define her because she stands firm in the truth that she is redeemed, loved, and called for a higher purpose.

A Heart Full of Grace and Forgiveness

Strength is not just about standing firm; it is also about showing grace, humility, and love. A strong woman, guided by God, does not carry bitterness or revenge in her heart. Instead, she chooses forgiveness, understanding that she, too, has been forgiven much (Ephesians 4:32). She leads with love, extending kindness even when it is undeserved,

"Decide today not to sit on your Greatness!"

and walks in peace knowing that vengeance belongs to the Lord (Romans 12:19).

Unmovable in Her Faith

No matter how fierce the storm, how deep the pain, or how long the waiting season, a strong woman refuses to be moved. She does not waver in her faith when prayers seem unanswered or when trials seem never-ending. She stands on the promises of God, knowing that His timing is perfect and that He is always faithful. Her trust in God is not circumstantial—it is absolute.

The Light That Inspires Others

A strong woman is not just strong for herself—she becomes a beacon of hope for others. Her unwavering faith, her endurance, and her peace in the midst of trials inspire those around her. She lifts others up, speaks life, and encourages them to stand firm in their own walk with God. She is a living testimony that strength is not about being invincible but about being completely dependent on God.

Conclusion

A strong woman finds her strength in God, and because of that, she will not be moved. She is a warrior in prayer,

"Decide today not to sit on your Greatness!"

a pillar of faith, and a light in the darkness. She faces life's battles with courage, knowing that victory is already hers through Christ. No matter what comes her way, she stands tall, knowing that God is her defender, her provider, and her unshakable foundation. **She will not be moved—because she stands in Him.**

"Decide today not to sit on your Greatness!"

"Greatness Awaits You!
There Is Nothing Impossible For You"

"Decide today not to sit on your Greatness!"

"Greatness Awaits You!
There Is Nothing Impossible For You"

"Decide today not to sit on your Greatness!"

Chapter 4

Always keeping your eyes on your greatness is key!

"Decide today not to sit on your Greatness!"

"Greatness Awaits You!
There Is Nothing Impossible For You"

"Always Keeping Your Eyes on
Your Greatness is Key!"

In a world filled with distractions, setbacks, and challenges, maintaining a steadfast focus on your greatness is essential for personal growth and success. Your greatness is the unique potential, purpose, and brilliance within you that can propel you to extraordinary heights. Whether you are pursuing your dreams, overcoming adversity, or striving for self-improvement, keeping your eyes fixed on your greatness is the key to unlocking your full potential.

Understanding Your Greatness:

Greatness is not just about talent, intelligence, or success—it is about embracing your unique qualities, passions, and the impact you can make in the world. Your greatness is found in:

Your Purpose – The reason you were created, the impact you are meant to have on others.

Your Resilience – The ability to rise above obstacles and challenges with determination.

Your Strengths – The skills, talents, and gifts that set you apart.

"Decide today not to sit on your Greatness!"

Your Mindset – The belief in yourself and your ability to achieve anything you set your heart to.

Your Growth – The continual pursuit of learning, evolving, and becoming the best version of yourself.

Why Keeping Your Eyes on Your Greatness is Important:

Overcoming Challenges – Life is full of setbacks, but focusing on your greatness helps you push through difficulties with confidence.

Staying Motivated – When you remind yourself of your potential, you remain inspired to keep going.

Avoiding Distractions – The world is filled with negativity, but keeping your eyes on your greatness allows you to block out anything that doesn't serve your purpose.

Building Confidence – Recognizing your greatness strengthens your belief in yourself and your abilities.

Achieving Success – True success comes from consistency, discipline, and keeping your vision aligned with your purpose.

"Decide today not to sit on your Greatness!"

"Greatness Awaits You!
There Is Nothing Impossible For You"

How to Keep Your Eyes on Your Greatness:

Know Your Worth – Remind yourself daily that you are valuable, capable, and worthy of success.

Set Clear Goals – Define what greatness looks like for you and set milestones to achieve it.

Surround Yourself with Positivity – Be around people who uplift and encourage you rather than bring you down.

Develop a Growth Mindset – Embrace challenges as opportunities to learn and grow rather than as obstacles.

Practice Gratitude – Recognize how far you have come and appreciate your journey.

Visualize Your Success – See yourself achieving your dreams, and let that vision drive you forward.

Stay Disciplined – Greatness requires consistency; build habits that support your vision.

Invest in Yourself – Take time to develop new skills, expand your knowledge, and improve daily.

Push Through Fear – Fear and doubt will arise, but courage is found in moving forward despite them.

"Decide today not to sit on your Greatness!"

Celebrate Your Progress – Every step forward is a victory; acknowledge and celebrate your wins, no matter how small.

Conclusion:

Your greatness is already within you—it is simply a matter of keeping your eyes on it. No matter what life throws your way, never lose sight of your potential, your dreams, and your purpose. Stay focused, stay determined, and always believe in the power of your own greatness. When you keep your eyes on your greatness, there is no limit to what you can achieve!

"Decide today not to sit on your Greatness!"

"Greatness Awaits You!
There Is Nothing Impossible For You"

"Decide today not to sit on your Greatness!"

"Greatness Awaits You!
There Is Nothing Impossible For You"

"Decide today not to sit on your Greatness!"

Chapter 5

Embrace and nurture your greatness daily!

"Decide today not to sit on your Greatness!"

"Greatness Awaits You!
There Is Nothing Impossible For You"

Hear, O Israel: the Lord our God is one Lord. And you shall love the Lord your God with all your heart and with your entire being with all your might.
Deuteronomy 6:4-5

Embrace and Nurture Your Greatness Daily:

Each of us has been created with a unique purpose, filled with talents, strengths, and potential that reflect the greatness placed within us by God. However, truly embracing and nurturing this greatness requires daily intention, faith, and discipline. It is not simply recognizing our gifts but actively using and developing them to make a positive impact in our lives and the lives of others.

Understanding Your Greatness:

Greatness is not measured by status, wealth, or external validation, but by our character, perseverance, and the way we align ourselves with our divine purpose. God has equipped each of us with unique abilities, wisdom, and a calling that we are meant to fulfill. To embrace our greatness, we must first understand that it is not based on comparison with others but rooted in our individual journey.

"Decide today not to sit on your Greatness!"

"Greatness Awaits You!
There Is Nothing Impossible For You"

Daily Practices to Nurture Your Greatness:

Start with Gratitude and Prayer

Each day is an opportunity to grow and walk in your greatness. Begin with gratitude, thanking God for another day and the gifts He has given you. Prayer and meditation help center your mind, align your spirit with God's purpose, and remind you that your greatness is a divine blessing.

Speak Life Over Yourself

The words we speak shape our mindset and actions. Replace negative self-talk with affirmations that align with your greatness:

I am fearfully and wonderfully made.

I am equipped to handle any challenge that comes my way.

I am walking in my purpose and fulfilling my divine calling.

Speaking life into yourself strengthens your confidence and faith.

Walk in Confidence, Not Fear

Fear and doubt can hinder us from fully embracing our potential. However, God has not given us a spirit of fear, but of power, love, and a sound mind (2 Timothy 1:7). Recognize fear as a temporary emotion, but do not allow it

"Decide today not to sit on your Greatness!"

to control your actions. Instead, move forward with faith, knowing that you are capable and prepared for the challenges ahead.

Develop and Use Your Gifts

Greatness is nurtured through continuous learning and growth. Identify your strengths and work on refining them. Whether it's in leadership, creativity, service, or problem-solving, commit to using your God-given abilities to serve others and make a difference.

Surround Yourself with People Who Uplift You

Your environment plays a crucial role in your growth. Stay connected to individuals who encourage, support, and challenge you to be the best version of yourself. Be intentional about building relationships that align with your purpose and elevate your potential.

Overcome Challenges with Faith

Life will present obstacles, but how you respond to them determines your growth. Instead of seeing difficulties as setbacks, view them as opportunities to strengthen your faith and resilience. Trust that every challenge is part of your journey to greater strength and wisdom.

Give Back and Serve Others

True greatness is not just about personal success but about using your gifts to uplift others. Whether through men-

"Decide today not to sit on your Greatness!"

torship, community service, or simply offering encouragement, impact those around you positively. When you pour into others, you also reinforce your own greatness.

Stay Committed to Personal Growth
Never stop learning, evolving, and refining yourself. Read, take courses, seek mentorship, and challenge yourself to grow spiritually, mentally, and emotionally. Invest in your personal development so that you can continue to walk in your greatness with confidence and wisdom.

Conclusion:
Walking Boldly in Your Greatness:

Embracing and nurturing your greatness is not a one-time decision but a daily practice. God has given you everything you need to be extraordinary—your talents, your faith, and your purpose. Each day, choose to walk boldly in that greatness, knowing that you are designed for impact, purpose, and success. Live with intention, uplift others, and trust that as you nurture your gifts, you will continue to evolve into the person God has created you to be.

Let your light shine daily and never dim
your greatness that is within you!

"Decide today not to sit on your Greatness!"

"Greatness Awaits You!
There Is Nothing Impossible For You"

"Decide today not to sit on your Greatness!"

"Greatness Awaits You!
There Is Nothing Impossible For You"

"Decide today not to sit on your Greatness!"

Chapter 6

"Don't Look Back, You're Not Going That Way!"

"Decide today not to sit on your Greatness!"

Life is a journey filled with twists, turns, challenges, and triumphs. As we move forward, it is natural to reflect on the past—on the mistakes we've made, the opportunities we've missed, and the people we've lost. However, dwelling on the past can prevent us from fully embracing the present and working towards the future we desire. The phrase *"Don't look back, you're not going that way"* is a powerful reminder that our focus should be on progress and growth, rather than regret and nostalgia.

The Meaning Behind the Phrase

This statement serves as both a metaphor and a motivational mantra. It encourages individuals to stop clinging to the past and instead direct their energy toward the future. While learning from past experiences is valuable, remaining stuck in them can hinder personal development and prevent us from realizing our full potential.

The Power of Forward Thinking

Just as a driver should focus on the road ahead rather than constantly checking the rearview mirror, we should channel our efforts into moving forward. Looking back too often can slow us down, cause us to second-guess ourselves, and create unnecessary anxiety. Instead, embracing forward-thinking allows us to:

"Decide today not to sit on your Greatness!"

"Greatness Awaits You!
There Is Nothing Impossible For You"

Set new goals and aspirations.

Focus on solutions rather than problems.

Develop resilience in the face of adversity.

Keep a positive outlook on life.

Letting Go of Regret

Regret can be a heavy burden, often weighing us down and making progress seem impossible. Whether it's a missed opportunity, a failed relationship, or a mistake, continually revisiting these moments only reinforces negative emotions. Instead of allowing regret to control our lives, we must:

Acknowledge past mistakes as learning experiences.

Forgive ourselves and others.

Redirect our energy toward creating a brighter future.

Understand that every experience—good or bad—shapes us into who we are today.

"Decide today not to sit on your Greatness!"

Overcoming Fear and Doubt

Fear of the unknown can make us hesitant to move forward. Many people hold onto the past because it feels familiar and comfortable, even when it no longer serves them. However, true growth requires stepping outside our comfort zones and embracing new opportunities. By refusing to look back, we:

Gain confidence in our abilities.

Break free from limiting beliefs.

Allow ourselves to take risks and embrace change.

Trust that the best is yet to come.

Practical Ways to Stop Looking Back

Understanding the importance of moving forward is one thing but putting it into practice requires conscious effort. Here are some actionable steps to help shift focus away from the past:

Practice Mindfulness

Mindfulness involves being fully present in the moment and appreciating life as it unfolds. By focusing on the now, we

"Decide today not to sit on your Greatness!"

can prevent our minds from drifting back to past regrets or future worries. Techniques such as meditation, deep breathing, and gratitude exercises can help cultivate mindfulness.

Set Clear Goals

Having a clear vision for the future provides direction and purpose. When we set achievable goals, our attention naturally shifts away from past failures and toward the steps necessary to reach our aspirations. Whether it's personal, professional, or emotional growth, defining specific objectives can help maintain forward momentum.

Surround Yourself with Positivity

The people we spend time with greatly influence our mindset. Being around those who encourage growth, inspire confidence, and offer support can make it easier to stay focused on the future. Conversely, distancing ourselves from toxic individuals who dwell on negativity can free us from the emotional weight of the past.

Accept That the Past Cannot Be Changed

One of the greatest lessons in life is accepting that no amount of regret can alter what has already happened. Instead of wishing for a different past, we should use those experiences to guide our decisions moving forward. Learning to

"Decide today not to sit on your Greatness!"

accept and appreciate the journey—flaws and all—can be incredibly liberating.

Take Action

Sometimes, the best way to move forward is simply to take action. Whether it's pursuing a new hobby, making a career change, or adopting a healthier lifestyle, taking even small steps toward self-improvement can be empowering. Progress, no matter how slow, is still progress.

Final Thoughts

"Don't look back, you're not going that way" is more than just a catchy phrase; it is a mindset that can transform the way we approach life. The past holds valuable lessons, but it should never become an anchor that prevents us from moving forward. By letting go of regret, overcoming fear, and embracing the future with confidence, we can create a life that is fulfilling, meaningful, and free from the chains of yesterday.

As we continue on our journey, let's remember that the road ahead is filled with endless possibilities. The past is a chapter that has already been written, but the future is a story waiting to be told. The choice is ours—will we keep looking back, or will we move boldly toward the destination we are meant to reach?

"Decide today not to sit on your Greatness!"

"Greatness Awaits You!
There Is Nothing Impossible For You"

"Decide today not to sit on your Greatness!"

"Greatness Awaits You!
There Is Nothing Impossible For You"

"Decide today not to sit on your Greatness!"

Chapter 7

Every great dream starts with a small one.

"Decide today not to sit on your Greatness!"

"Greatness Awaits You!
There Is Nothing Impossible For You"

The Power of Small Beginnings

Dreams are the foundation of achievement. Every great invention, business, movement, or personal success story begins with a single, small idea. The phrase *"Every great dream starts with a small one"* highlights the significance of humble beginnings and the gradual process of growth, development, and perseverance that leads to success.

The Seed of a Dream:

Like a seed planted in the ground, dreams start small. A single thought, vision, or passion sparks the possibility of something greater. Many of the world's most remarkable achievements—whether in science, technology, business, or the arts—were initially just ideas in someone's mind. Walt Disney's empire began with a sketch of a simple character, Steve Jobs and Steve Wozniak started Apple in a garage, and great leaders throughout history began with a single step toward their vision.

The Power of Taking Small Steps:

One of the biggest reasons many dreams never come to fruition is the fear of starting small. People often want to leap directly into greatness, but the truth is that success is built through a series of small, consistent actions. Every great entrepreneur, artist, athlete, or leader understands that

"Decide today not to sit on your Greatness!"

mastery takes time. Small steps build momentum, allowing individuals to refine their skills, adapt to challenges, and develop resilience.

For example, an aspiring writer may begin with a journal, a single poem, or a blog post before publishing a book. A young athlete might start training in a local gym before becoming a champion. A future business mogul may first learn to manage their personal finances before launching a multi-million-dollar company.

Patience and Persistence:

Dreams do not materialize overnight. The road from a small dream to a great one is filled with setbacks, obstacles, and doubts. However, those who stay committed to their vision and persist despite challenges eventually see their dreams grow into something remarkable. It is essential to nurture a dream with patience, just as a gardener waters a seed, knowing it will take time to sprout and flourish.

Embracing Growth and Learning:

Small beginnings provide the opportunity to learn, experiment, and improve. Mistakes and failures along the way serve as valuable lessons that shape the dreamer's journey. Growth happens incrementally, and each step taken brings a person closer to their ultimate goal.

"Decide today not to sit on your Greatness!"

Inspiring Others:

One of the most beautiful aspects of starting small is that it inspires others. When people see someone transform a small dream into something impactful, it gives them hope that they, too, can achieve greatness. Whether it's an individual pursuing personal goals or a leader building a movement, every great dream has the power to influence and uplift others.

Conclusion:

"Every great dream starts with a small one" is a reminder that all significant achievements have humble beginnings. By taking small, consistent steps, staying patient, learning from experiences, and persevering through challenges, anyone can transform their dream into reality. No dream is too small to matter, and every step forward brings it closer to greatness. So, dare to dream, start where you are, and trust the process—because what begins as a simple idea today can change the world tomorrow.

"Decide today not to sit on your Greatness!"

"Greatness Awaits You!
There Is Nothing Impossible For You"

"Decide today not to sit on your Greatness!"

"Greatness Awaits You!
There Is Nothing Impossible For You"

"Decide today not to sit on your Greatness!"

Chapter 8

Faith Is the Title Deed to Your Greatness

"Decide today not to sit on your Greatness!"

"Greatness Awaits You! There Is Nothing Impossible For You"

Faith is often described as belief in the unseen, a deep conviction that something exists or will come to pass even when there is no physical evidence to support it. But faith is more than just belief—it is the **title deed** to your greatness. Just as a title deed is proof of ownership of property, faith is the assurance that your dreams, potential, and purpose are already yours, waiting to be realized.

Understanding Faith as a Title Deed

A title deed is a legal document that proves you own something, whether it is land, a home, or a business. It means that regardless of whether you can physically touch or see the property at any given moment, it belongs to you. In the same way, **faith is the divine title deed** to your God-given destiny. Even when your greatness is not yet visible, faith confirms that it already exists in the spiritual realm and will manifest in due time.

Hebrews 11:1 (AMP) states:
"Now faith is the assurance (title deed, confirmation) of things hoped for (divinely guaranteed), and the evidence of things not seen (the conviction of their reality—faith comprehends as fact what cannot be experienced by the physical senses)."

This verse reveals that faith is not just wishful thinking; it is a **spiritual contract** that guarantees access to the promises and greatness God has designed for you.

"Decide today not to sit on your Greatness!"

Faith and Your Greatness

Greatness is not just about success, wealth, or recognition. True greatness is fulfilling the purpose for which you were created. It is walking in divine alignment with your calling, impacting lives, and leaving a legacy. However, the road to greatness is rarely easy—it requires persistence, resilience, and an unwavering trust in God's promises.

Faith acts as the title deed by:

1. **Granting Ownership of Your Destiny** – Even before success materializes, faith confirms that your greatness is already yours. You don't have to wait for external validation because faith secures it in advance.
2. **Overcoming Obstacles** – Challenges, failures, and delays may come, but faith assures you that your purpose is intact, just as a title deed confirms ownership even if a property is under construction.
3. **Fueling Action** – Just as someone with a title deed is confident to step onto their property and build, faith gives you the courage to take steps toward your destiny, knowing it belongs to you.
4. **Defying Fear and Doubt** – When others question your journey, faith reminds you that your greatness is already established in the spiritual realm. It is not a matter of *if* but *when*.

"Decide today not to sit on your Greatness!"

Living as If You Already Own It

A person who has a title deed to a house does not worry about whether the house is real; they know it is theirs. Likewise, when you walk in faith, you carry yourself with confidence, speak with conviction, and make decisions based on the certainty that your greatness is already secured. You do not need to see the full picture to believe; you simply need to trust the One who holds the blueprint of your life.

Conclusion

Faith is not just about believing—it is about knowing. It is the title deed that confirms your destiny, your greatness, and your divine purpose. When you activate faith, you step into your inheritance with boldness, understanding that nothing can take away what God has already assigned to you. Keep believing, keep building, and keep walking in the confidence that **your greatness is already yours!**

"Decide today not to sit on your Greatness!"

"Greatness Awaits You!
There Is Nothing Impossible For You"

"Decide today not to sit on your Greatness!"

"Greatness Awaits You!
There Is Nothing Impossible For You"

"Decide today not to sit on your Greatness!"

Chapter 9

"God Created You with Greatness in Mind!"

"Decide today not to sit on your Greatness!"

"Greatness Awaits You!
There Is Nothing Impossible For You"

From the very beginning, God designed each of us with a unique purpose, a special destiny, and an undeniable greatness that is woven into the fabric of our being. You are not an accident or an afterthought; you are the intentional creation of a God who sees value, potential, and significance in you. He formed you with love, equipped you with talents, and placed within you the seeds of greatness.

1. Created in His Image

The Bible tells us in **Genesis 1:27**, "So God created man in His own image, in the image of God He created him; male and female He created them." This means that you were made to reflect the character, creativity, and power of God. You carry within you the imprint of divine greatness, and that alone makes you extraordinary.

2. You Are Fearfully and Wonderfully Made

Psalm 139:14 declares, **"I praise You because I am fearfully and wonderfully made; Your works are wonderful, I know that full well."** This verse is a powerful reminder that you are crafted with precision, care, and intention. Every detail about you—your gifts, your abilities, your personality—was designed by God for a reason. He sees greatness in you, even when you don't see it in yourself.

"Decide today not to sit on your Greatness!"

3. You Have a Purpose

God never creates anything without purpose. **Jeremiah 29:11** assures us, **"For I know the plans I have for you, declares the Lord, plans to prosper you and not to harm you, plans to give you a future and a hope."** You were created with a mission, an assignment that only you can fulfill. Your experiences, strengths, and even your struggles are part of a greater plan designed to shape you into the person God has called you to be.

4. You Are Empowered for Greatness

God does not just call you to greatness—He equips you for it. **2 Timothy 1:7** says, **"For God has not given us a spirit of fear, but of power and of love and of a sound mind."** You are not weak, incapable, or unworthy. You have the power of God working within you, enabling you to rise above challenges, impact lives, and fulfill your divine purpose.

5. You Were Born to Overcome

Life may present obstacles, but you were designed to conquer them. **Romans 8:37** reminds us, **"No, in all these things we are more than conquerors through Him who loved us."** The greatness in you is not limited by circumstances, hardships, or mistakes. God's grace covers you; His strength sustains you, and His favor goes before you.

"Decide today not to sit on your Greatness!"

6. Walking in Your Greatness

To fully embrace the greatness God has placed within you:

Seek Him Daily – Develop a relationship with God through prayer, worship, and reading His Word.

Discover Your Gifts – Identify your talents and passions, as they are clues to your divine purpose.

Step Out in Faith – Trust God and take bold steps toward your calling.

Surround Yourself with Encouragement – Stay connected to people who uplift, inspire, and challenge you to grow.

Give Back – Use your gifts to serve others, knowing that greatness is not just about what you achieve but how you impact lives.

Conclusion

God created you with greatness in mind—not by the world's definition, but by His divine design. Your worth is not measured by what you have, where you come from, or what you have done, but by who you are in Christ. He has equipped you, empowered you, and set you apart for some-

"Decide today not to sit on your Greatness!"

thing extraordinary. Never doubt your value, never shrink back in fear, and never settle for less than what God has destined for you.

You were born to be great. Walk in it!

"Decide today not to sit on your Greatness!"

"Greatness Awaits You!
There Is Nothing Impossible For You"

"Decide today not to sit on your Greatness!"

"Greatness Awaits You!
There Is Nothing Impossible For You"

"Decide today not to sit on your Greatness!"

Chapter 10

"God will close doors when It Is time for us to move forward. He knows that we will not move unless our circumstances force us to!"

"Decide today not to sit on your Greatness!"

"Greatness Awaits You!
There Is Nothing Impossible For You"

Life is full of transitions, and often, the most significant growth comes through moments of discomfort, uncertainty, and even loss. One of the most profound ways God guides us is by closing doors—removing opportunities, relationships, or situations that we have become too comfortable with. While this can be painful and confusing at the moment, it is often the catalyst for our greatest breakthroughs.

Divine Disruptions for Greater Purpose

God understands human nature. We are creatures of habit, and we often resist change, even when it is necessary for our growth. We cling to familiarity, routines, and comfort zones, not realizing that they may be holding us back. Because of this, God sometimes allows circumstances to shift in a way that forces us to move forward.

- **Blocked Opportunities:** What we see as a rejection, or a missed chance is often God's redirection. We may not understand why a job offer was withdrawn, a business failed, or a relationship ended, but these closed doors are often divine setups for something better.
- **Shaken Comfort Zones:** When life is going smoothly, we may not see a reason to step into new territory. But when God wants us to grow, He sometimes removes our comfort, making it clear that it is time to move forward.

"Decide today not to sit on your Greatness!"

- **Unanswered Prayers:** Sometimes, we pray for a door to remain open, but God, in His infinite wisdom, allows it to close. While it may seem like a denial, it is often divine protection or preparation for a greater blessing.

Biblical Examples of God Closing Doors Throughout scripture, we see examples of God closing doors to propel His people into their divine destinies:

The Israelites Leaving Egypt (Exodus 14) – The Israelites were enslaved in Egypt for generations. Even when God sent Moses to lead them out, Pharaoh refused to let them go until God sent plagues to force the change. The Red Sea was a closed door that seemed impossible to cross, but God miraculously made a way.

Elijah at the Brook (1 Kings 17:7-9) – God provided water and food for Elijah at the Brook Cherith during a drought. But when the brook dried up, it was a sign that it was time for Elijah to move to Zarephath, where God had prepared a widow to provide for him.

Paul's Missionary Journey (Acts 16:6-10) – Paul and his companions planned to preach in Asia, but the Holy Spirit prevented them from going. They later received a vision directing them to Macedonia, where their ministry flourished.

"Decide today not to sit on your Greatness!"

These examples illustrate that when one door closes, it is not the end—it's a divine transition leading to something greater.

Trusting God Through Closed Doors

It is natural to feel disappointed, frustrated, or even fearful when a door closes. However, instead of seeing it as a setback, we should view it as God's way of guiding us into something better. Here's how we can navigate closed doors with faith:

Seek God's Guidance – When faced with a closed door, turn to God in prayer. Ask Him to reveal the next steps and trust that He is leading you.

Let Go of the Past – Holding on to what is familiar can prevent you from embracing new opportunities. Release the past and trust that God's plan is always for your good.

Stay Open to New Opportunities – God often brings new doors into our lives that we never expected. Stay open to change and be willing to step into new directions with faith.

Trust the Timing – Just because a door is closed now doesn't mean it's closed forever. Some doors reopen in God's perfect timing, while others remain shut for our protection.

"Decide today not to sit on your Greatness!"

Conclusion

God's ways are higher than ours, and He sees what we cannot. When He closes a door, it is not to harm us but to move us into the next phase of our purpose. If we were left to our own choices, we might remain stagnant, settling for less than what God has prepared for us. But in His love and wisdom, He removes what no longer serves us, pushing us toward our destiny.

Instead of resisting closed doors, we should embrace them with faith, knowing that God is positioning us for greater opportunities, growth, and blessings. Every closed door is a divine invitation to step into something new.

"Decide today not to sit on your Greatness!"

"Greatness Awaits You!
There Is Nothing Impossible For You"

"Decide today not to sit on your Greatness!"

"Greatness Awaits You!
There Is Nothing Impossible For You"

"Decide today not to sit on your Greatness!"

Chapter 11

"Great Things Happen When You Have Great Expectations!"

"Decide today not to sit on your Greatness!"

"Greatness Awaits You!
There Is Nothing Impossible For You"

"Great Things Happen When You Have Great Expectations!" is a powerful affirmation that speaks to the transformative power of mindset, vision, and belief. This phrase encapsulates the idea that when individuals set high standards for themselves and cultivate a mindset of expectation, they naturally align their actions and efforts toward success. It serves as a motivational statement that encourages people to dream big, work hard, and persist in the face of challenges.

The Power of Expectation

Expectations are more than mere thoughts—they are deeply held beliefs that shape our reality. When a person genuinely expects great things, they operate with a level of confidence and determination that increases the likelihood of achieving their goals. This principle is evident in various aspects of life, including:

Personal Growth & Development

High expectations push individuals to become the best version of themselves.

Self-discipline, commitment, and perseverance become natural habits.

"Decide today not to sit on your Greatness!"

"Greatness Awaits You!
There Is Nothing Impossible For You"

Positive expectations create a mindset of continuous learning and self-improvement.

Professional Success

Employees and entrepreneurs who expect success are more proactive and solution oriented.

Leaders with great expectations inspire teams to achieve excellence.

Goal-setting and strategic planning become crucial when working toward ambitious outcomes.

Relationships & Community Impact

Expecting the best from relationships leads to stronger, healthier connections.

Leaders who expect positive change within their communities take action to create it.

Social movements and major advancements are often fueled by individuals who believe in a better future.

"Decide today not to sit on your Greatness!"

"Greatness Awaits You!
There Is Nothing Impossible For You"

Faith & Resilience

Faith-driven individuals understand that expectations, combined with action, lead to transformation.

Believing in a higher purpose allows individuals to navigate adversity with strength.

A positive outlook on life reinforces the ability to overcome obstacles and challenges.

Practical Ways to Cultivate Great Expectations

To see great things happen in life, one must be intentional about fostering a mindset of expectation. Some practical steps include:

Visualization: Envision success and mentally experience achieving your goals.

Affirmations: Speak positive words over your life daily to reinforce belief.

Action-Oriented Goal Setting: Define clear, actionable steps that lead toward your aspirations.

"Decide today not to sit on your Greatness!"

"Greatness Awaits You!
There Is Nothing Impossible For You"

Surrounding Yourself with Excellence: Engage with mentors, leaders, and peers who embody high expectations.

Faith & Persistence: Maintain faith in your journey and be persistent, even when faced with setbacks.

Conclusion

The statement **"Great Things Happen When You Have Great Expectations!"** is more than just a motivational phrase—it is a mindset, a call to action, and a way of life. By fostering high expectations and backing them up with commitment, resilience, and strategic effort, individuals can manifest remarkable outcomes in their personal lives, careers, and communities. When you truly expect greatness, you set the stage for extraordinary achievements!

"Decide today not to sit on your Greatness!"

"Greatness Awaits You!
There Is Nothing Impossible For You"

"Decide today not to sit on your Greatness!"

"Greatness Awaits You!
There Is Nothing Impossible For You"

"Decide today not to sit on your Greatness!"

Chapter 12

Greatness Awaits You

"Decide today not to sit on your Greatness!"

"Greatness Awaits You!
There Is Nothing Impossible For You"

Reflection on Jeremiah 29:11:

"For I know the plans I have for you," declares the Lord, "plans to prosper you and not to harm you, plans to give you hope and a future."

Jeremiah 29:11 is a scripture that brings comfort, encouragement, and reassurance. It reminds us that God has a divine purpose for each of our lives, filled with hope and a bright future. In this verse, God speaks through the prophet Jeremiah to the Israelites who were in exile in Babylon. They were enduring hardship and uncertainty, yet God assured them that He had not forgotten them and that His plans for them were good and full of promise.

This verse is a declaration of God's sovereignty, love, and faithfulness. It assures us that no matter the challenges we face, God's plans for us are rooted in His goodness and desire for us to thrive. It is a reminder that our circumstances do not define our destiny, and the trials we endure are often a preparation for the greatness that lies ahead.

Greatness Awaits You Journal:
A Journey of Discovery

The "Greatness Awaits You Journal" is inspired by the truth of Jeremiah 29:11, serving as a daily reminder that God has

"Decide today not to sit on your Greatness!"

incredible plans in store for you. Through this journal, my prayer is that you will:

1. **Discover the Greatness Within You**
   Greatness is not something external that you must chase—it already resides inside you. God has uniquely equipped you with talents, gifts, and purpose. As you reflect on your journey and document your thoughts in this journal, may you come to see the seeds of greatness that God has planted within you.

2. **Embrace God's Plans with Faith**
   Jeremiah 29:11 assures us that God's plans are to prosper us, not to harm us. Even when life feels uncertain, trust that God is working behind the scenes for your good. Use this journal as a place to write down your dreams, prayers, and the ways you see God moving in your life. Let it be a tool to build your faith in His perfect timing.

3. **Step Boldly into Hope and Your Future**
   Hope is a powerful force that fuels our belief in better days ahead. This journal is a space for you to record moments of hope, victories big and small, and steps you take toward your God-given future. Let it remind you that God's plans for you are full of promise and potential.

4. **Overcome Challenges with Confidence**

"Decide today not to sit on your Greatness!"

"Greatness Awaits You!
There Is Nothing Impossible For You"

Life's difficulties can sometimes overshadow our view of God's promises. Use this journal as a means to process your challenges and renew your confidence in God's Word. Remember, His plans are never to harm you but to shape you into the person He created you to be.

A Blessing for Your Journey

My hope is that the "Greatness Awaits You Journal" becomes more than just a book but a companion on your journey to discovering the fullness of God's purpose for your life. May it serve as a constant reminder that greatness truly awaits you because you are loved, chosen, and destined for extraordinary things.

Let this verse guide you:

"And we know that in all things God works for the good of those who love him, who have been called according to his purpose." —Romans 8:28

May you walk boldly in the knowledge that God's plans for your life are filled with prosperity, hope, and a beautiful future. Greatness is within you, and the best is yet to come!

"Decide today not to sit on your Greatness!"

"Greatness Awaits You!
There Is Nothing Impossible For You"

"Decide today not to sit on your Greatness!"

"Greatness Awaits You!
There Is Nothing Impossible For You"

"Decide today not to sit on your Greatness!"

Chapter 13

Greatness cost and there is no clearance, Price!

"Decide today not to sit on your Greatness!"

God Paid the Ultimate Price for Us

The magnitude of God's love for us is revealed in the ultimate price He paid through the sacrifice of His Son, Jesus Christ. This act was not cheap—it was the most profound demonstration of love and grace. It came at the cost of unimaginable suffering, humility, and death. In John 3:16, we are reminded of this truth: *"For God so loved the world that He gave His only begotten Son, that whoever believes in Him should not perish but have everlasting life."* This gift of salvation is freely given to us, but its cost was immense—a reminder of the depth of God's commitment to us.

The Cost of Success in God's Plan

Just as God paid a price for our redemption, there is a price we must pay to achieve the success He desires for us. While salvation is a free gift, walking in His purpose and fulfilling His plan for our lives requires effort, sacrifice, and faithfulness. Success in God's eyes is not about worldly riches or status but about aligning our lives with His will, growing in character, and fulfilling the unique mission He has given each of us.

The Price We Must Pay

Sacrifice of Self
To live in alignment with God's plan, we must deny ourselves and take up our cross daily (Luke 9:23). This means

"Decide today not to sit on your Greatness!"

99

putting aside our selfish desires and ambitions to pursue His will. Success often requires letting go of comfort, convenience, and worldly pleasures to focus on His purpose.

Obedience to His Word

True success requires obedience. In Joshua 1:8, God instructs us to meditate on His Word day and night and to obey it so that we may be prosperous and successful. This involves discipline, study, and a heart willing to follow His commandments.

Faith and Perseverance

Walking in God's purpose often means enduring challenges, trials, and setbacks. Hebrews 11 speaks of heroes of faith who paid the price of perseverance, trusting God's promises even when the path seemed unclear. Success demands unwavering faith and the courage to keep moving forward despite obstacles.

Commitment to Serving Others

Jesus exemplified servant leadership, showing us that greatness comes through serving others (Mark 10:45). Paying the price for success in God's kingdom involves investing in the lives of others, putting their needs above our own, and reflecting Christ's love through our actions.

"Decide today not to sit on your Greatness!"

Time and Effort

Success in God's plan is not instantaneous; it requires time, effort, and dedication. Whether it's developing our gifts, growing in spiritual maturity, or pursuing a God-given vision, we must be willing to work diligently and remain patient as He unfolds His plans for us.

The Rewards of Paying the Price

Though the cost of following God's plan may seem high, the rewards are eternal and incomparable. In Matthew 16:25-26, Jesus reminds us that gaining the whole world means nothing if we lose our soul. Conversely, when we invest in God's kingdom, we reap rewards that cannot be destroyed (Matthew 6:19-21). The price we pay now is a small sacrifice compared to the joy, peace, and eternal inheritance we receive in Christ.

Final Encouragement

Let us remember that the ultimate price has already been paid by Jesus. Our responsibility is to honor His sacrifice by living lives that glorify Him and pursuing the success He desires for us. While the journey may be challenging, we can take heart in knowing that God is with us every step of the way. His grace empowers us to pay the price, and His promises assure us that our labor in Him is never in vain (1 Corinthians 15:58).

"Decide today not to sit on your Greatness!"

"Greatness Awaits You!
There Is Nothing Impossible For You"

"Decide today not to sit on your Greatness!"

"Greatness Awaits You!
There Is Nothing Impossible For You"

"Decide today not to sit on your Greatness!"

Chapter 14

"Having faith in God's power is key even when you can't trace Him."

"Decide today not to sit on your Greatness!"

"Greatness Awaits You!
There Is Nothing Impossible For You"

Life is filled with moments of uncertainty, challenges, and trials that test the very foundation of our faith. There are times when it seems as though God is silent, absent, or even distant. However, as believers, we are called to trust in God's power, even when we cannot see His hand at work. The essence of faith is not in knowing every step of the journey but in trusting the One who holds the future.

Faith in God's Power: A Biblical Foundation

Hebrews 11:1 defines faith as "the substance of things hoped for, the evidence of things not seen." This means that faith is not based on what we can physically see but on the assurance of God's promises. Throughout Scripture, there are countless examples of individuals who had to trust in God even when they could not trace His presence:

Abraham's Journey of Faith – God called Abraham to leave his homeland and go to a place He would later reveal (Genesis 12:1-4). Abraham had no map, no clear direction, yet he obeyed because he trusted in God's power and faithfulness.

Joseph's Season of Trials – Joseph was sold into slavery, falsely accused, and imprisoned (Genesis 37-50). For years, it seemed as though God had forgotten him, yet he remained faithful. In the end, he saw how God had orchestrated everything for His divine purpose.

"Decide today not to sit on your Greatness!"

Job's Unshakable Trust – Job lost everything—his wealth, health, and even his children. Though he did not understand why he was suffering, he declared, *"Though He slay me, yet will I trust in Him"* (Job 13:15). His story reminds us that faith is not about our circumstances but about our confidence in God.

Why Faith in God's Power is Key

God is Always at Work, Even When We Can't See Him

Just because we cannot trace God does not mean He is absent. Often, God works behind the scenes, aligning circumstances for our good. Romans 8:28 assures us that *"all things work together for good to those who love God, to those who are called according to His purpose."*

Faith Requires Trust, Not Sight

Faith is not about seeing but about believing. If we could always see the outcome, faith would not be necessary. Jesus told Thomas, *"Blessed are those who have not seen and yet have believed"* (John 20:29). God calls us to trust Him even when we have no visible proof of His presence.

God's Timing is Perfect

Often, we become impatient when God does not act immediately. However, His timing is always perfect. Isaiah 55:8-9 reminds us that His ways are higher than ours. What seems like a delay is often God's preparation.

"Decide today not to sit on your Greatness!"

Faith Produces Strength and Endurance
Trials and uncertainties are part of the Christian journey, but faith in God's power helps us endure. James 1:3-4 says that the testing of our faith produces perseverance, leading us to spiritual maturity.

Faith Opens Doors to Miracles
In Matthew 17:20, Jesus declares that even faith as small as a mustard seed can move mountains. God responds to faith, and when we trust in His power, we position ourselves to receive His miraculous intervention.

How to Strengthen Your Faith When You Can't Trace God

Anchor Yourself in God's Word – The Bible is filled with promises that remind us of God's faithfulness. Regularly reading and meditating on Scripture strengthens our faith.

Remember Past Victories – Reflecting on how God has come through in the past helps us trust Him for the future.

Surround Yourself with Faithful Believers – Being part of a strong faith community encourages us to remain steadfast even in difficult times.

"Decide today not to sit on your Greatness!"

Pray Without Ceasing – Prayer is not just about asking God for help but about deepening our relationship with Him.

Praise God in Advance – Worship shifts our focus from problems to God's greatness. Even when we can't see Him working, praising Him acknowledges that He is in control.

Conclusion

Faith in God's power is the key to navigating the uncertainties of life. Even when we cannot trace Him, we can trust that He is working behind the scenes for our good. Like Abraham, Joseph, and Job, we must hold on to faith, believing that God is sovereign and faithful. When we walk by faith and not by sight (2 Corinthians 5:7), we position ourselves for divine breakthroughs, knowing that God is always in control, even in the unseen.

So, when life's trials make you feel lost, remember this: God is never absent. His silence does not mean His absence, and His delay is never His denial. Keep trusting, keep believing, and keep walking in faith—because God is always working, even when you can't trace Him.

"Decide today not to sit on your Greatness!"

"Greatness Awaits You!
There Is Nothing Impossible For You"

"Decide today not to sit on your Greatness!"

"Greatness Awaits You!
There Is Nothing Impossible For You"

"Decide today not to sit on your Greatness!"

Chapter 15

"I Will Learn from My Past Because It Will Prepare Me for My Future!"

Life is a journey filled with experiences, both good and bad. The past holds valuable lessons that shape who we are and guide us toward who we are becoming. While some may see the past as a place of regret or nostalgia, it is truly a foundation of wisdom that prepares us for what lies ahead. Embracing the lessons from our past ensures that we do not repeat mistakes, that we grow stronger from challenges, and that we use our experiences to create a better future.

Understanding the Role of the Past

The past is a teacher. Every failure, success, challenge, and victory contributes to our understanding of life. Mistakes teach us what doesn't work, while achievements show us what we are capable of. Our past experiences provide clarity on what truly matters, helping us make better decisions in the present and future.

For example, if we have experienced failure in relationships, careers, or personal growth, we can analyze what went wrong and how we can do things differently moving forward. If we have succeeded in certain areas, we can reflect on what habits or choices led to those accomplishments and replicate them in the future.

"Decide today not to sit on your Greatness!"

"Greatness Awaits You!
There Is Nothing Impossible For You"

Learning from Mistakes

Mistakes are often seen as setbacks, but in reality, they are stepping stones to success. Every error we make provides an opportunity to learn and improve. Instead of dwelling on what went wrong, we should ask ourselves:

What led to this mistake?

What can I do differently next time?

How can this experience make me wiser?

By answering these questions, we shift our mindset from regret to growth. People who refuse to learn from their mistakes often find themselves repeating the same cycles. However, those who take the time to reflect and adjust their actions gain the wisdom needed to move forward with confidence.

Overcoming Challenges and Adversity

Life's difficulties are not meant to break us but to build us. Hard times strengthen our resilience, teach us patience, and help us develop a deeper understanding of life. When we go through hardships, we gain insights that prepare us for future obstacles.

"Decide today not to sit on your Greatness!"

For example, someone who has faced financial struggles may learn the importance of saving, budgeting, and financial planning. A person who has experienced heartbreak may develop emotional strength and better judgment when choosing relationships in the future. The key is to see challenges not as roadblocks but as stepping stones to personal and professional growth.

Applying Lessons to the Future

Once we recognize the lessons our past has taught us, it is crucial to apply them. It is not enough to acknowledge mistakes or hardships; we must use our experiences to make better choices moving forward. This can be done by:

Setting goals based on past experiences

Making wiser decisions to avoid previous pitfalls

Developing new habits that lead to personal growth

Seeking mentorship or guidance from those who have learned similar lessons

By using our past as a guide, we position ourselves for a brighter and more successful future.

"Decide today not to sit on your Greatness!"

Letting Go of the Past While Learning from It

While learning from the past is essential, it is equally important to avoid being trapped by it. Some people allow past failures, guilt, or pain to define them, preventing them from moving forward. Instead of seeing the past as a prison, we should see it as a classroom. The key is to take the lessons and move forward with hope, confidence, and a renewed sense of purpose.

Conclusion

The past is a valuable tool for preparing us for the future. It teaches us lessons, strengthens our character, and provides wisdom that helps us make better choices. By learning from our mistakes, overcoming challenges, and applying the knowledge we've gained, we create a future that is guided by wisdom and experience. Instead of fearing or regretting the past, we should embrace it as a stepping stone to a brighter and more fulfilling life.

"Decide today not to sit on your Greatness!"

"Greatness Awaits You!
There Is Nothing Impossible For You"

"Decide today not to sit on your Greatness!"

"Greatness Awaits You!
There Is Nothing Impossible For You"

"Decide today not to sit on your Greatness!"

Chapter 16

"If You Are Not Moving Forward, You Are Standing Still – Which Means You Are Headed Nowhere!"

"Decide today not to sit on your Greatness!"

"Greatness Awaits You!
There Is Nothing Impossible For You"

Life is a journey, and progress is essential for growth and success. The phrase **"If you are not moving forward, you are standing still, which means you are headed nowhere"** serves as a powerful reminder that stagnation leads to missed opportunities and unfulfilled potential. Whether in personal development, career aspirations, relationships, or business, continuous movement and improvement are necessary to achieve success and fulfillment.

Understanding the Concept of Forward Movement

Forward movement signifies progress, learning, and development. It doesn't always mean drastic or rapid changes, but rather consistent steps toward a goal, dream, or purpose. Progress can take many forms:

Self-Improvement: Acquiring new knowledge, refining skills, and adapting to change.

Career Growth: Seeking advancement, learning from challenges, and embracing innovation.

Emotional and Mental Growth: Overcoming fears, strengthening resilience, and practicing self-awareness.

Spiritual Growth: Deepening faith, mindfulness, and understanding of one's purpose.

"Decide today not to sit on your Greatness!"

When individuals or organizations stop striving for progress, they become stagnant, and stagnation often leads to decline.

The Dangers of Standing Still

Standing still may feel comfortable because it eliminates risk and effort. However, this comfort zone is deceptive because the world is constantly changing. When you fail to progress, you don't just stay in the same place—you actually fall behind. Here's why:

The World Doesn't Wait for You

In every aspect of life, change is constant. Technology advances, industries evolve, social norms shift, and economies fluctuate. If you refuse to adapt and grow, you risk becoming outdated or irrelevant. Businesses that fail to innovate often collapse, and individuals who refuse to learn new skills struggle in their careers.

Fear of Failure Leads to Missed Opportunities

One of the main reasons people remain stagnant is fear—fear of failure, rejection, or the unknown. However, standing still is often a greater risk than moving forward because it leads to regret and missed opportunities. Even if progress

"Decide today not to sit on your Greatness!"

involves making mistakes, those mistakes teach valuable lessons that contribute to future success.

Stagnation Breeds Discontent and Regret

When you don't challenge yourself to grow, you may begin to feel unfulfilled. People who refuse to push themselves often experience boredom, dissatisfaction, and even depression. Progress brings excitement, motivation, and a sense of purpose.

Relationships and Networks Require Effort

Just like personal growth, relationships also need continuous effort and nurturing. Whether it's friendships, romantic relationships, or professional networks, standing still in these areas can lead to distance, miscommunication, and disconnection.

Lack of Movement Can Lead to Decline

Not progressing doesn't mean staying at the same level indefinitely—it often leads to decline. In fitness, if you stop exercising, your strength and endurance weaken. In business, if a company stops evolving, it eventually gets outperformed by competitors. In life, if you stop growing, you risk losing opportunities for happiness and success.

"Decide today not to sit on your Greatness!"

How to Keep Moving Forward

If you find yourself stuck or unmotivated, there are ways to break free from stagnation and move forward:

1. **Set Clear Goals**

Define what you want to achieve and break your goals into actionable steps. Having a roadmap gives you direction and helps you stay motivated.

2. **Embrace Continuous Learning**

Never stop acquiring knowledge and new skills. Read books, take courses, seek mentorship, and stay open to new experiences.

3. **Step Out of Your Comfort Zone**

Growth happens when you challenge yourself. Take risks, try new things, and embrace uncertainty. Even small steps outside your comfort zone can create big changes.

4. **Take Action, Even in Small Ways**

Waiting for the "perfect moment" often leads to inaction. Start where you are with what you have. Progress, no matter how small, is still movement.

"Decide today not to sit on your Greatness!"

5. **Surround Yourself with Motivated People**

The people around you influence your mindset. Engage with individuals who encourage growth, challenge you to improve, and push you to move forward.

6. **Learn from Setbacks**

Failure and mistakes are part of the journey. Instead of allowing them to keep you stagnant, use them as learning opportunities. Every setback contains a lesson that can propel you forward.

7. **Stay Adaptable and Open to Change**

Flexibility is key to growth. Be willing to adjust your strategies, try new approaches, and accept that change is necessary for success.

Final Thoughts

The choice to move forward or stand still ultimately determines the direction of your life. Those who consistently strive for progress, challenge themselves, and embrace change achieve greater success and fulfillment. Standing still may feel safe, but it leads nowhere. Growth requires effort, but it is the only path to reaching your full potential.

"Decide today not to sit on your Greatness!"

"Greatness Awaits You!
There Is Nothing Impossible For You"

Don't let fear, comfort, or complacency keep you from moving forward. Take action today, embrace challenges, and continuously strive for improvement—because standing still is not an option.

"Decide today not to sit on your Greatness!"

"Greatness Awaits You!
There Is Nothing Impossible For You"

"Decide today not to sit on your Greatness!"

"Greatness Awaits You!
There Is Nothing Impossible For You"

"Decide today not to sit on your Greatness!"

Chapter 17

"If you do not move in the direction of your greatness, it will leave to behind."

"Decide today not to sit on your Greatness!"

"Greatness Awaits You! There Is Nothing Impossible For You"

This statement is a powerful reminder that personal growth and success are not automatic; they require intentional effort, action, and movement. Greatness is not something that waits for anyone. It is an evolving force that exists within every individual, but if one does not actively pursue it, it will pass them by, leaving them in a state of stagnation and regret.

Understanding Greatness

Greatness is the fulfillment of one's potential, the manifestation of purpose, and the realization of one's highest abilities. It is the journey toward excellence, self-improvement, and making a meaningful impact in one's life and the lives of others. Greatness does not come from standing still; it requires action, perseverance, and resilience.

Every person is born with unique talents, gifts, and opportunities. However, if those talents are not nurtured, if those gifts are not developed, and if opportunities are ignored, greatness becomes a distant dream rather than a lived reality. It is not enough to simply have potential; one must actively engage in personal and professional growth to bring that potential to life.

"Decide today not to sit on your Greatness!"

The Consequence of Inaction

If an individual chooses not to move forward, they risk being left behind by their own aspirations. Here's how inaction can cause greatness to slip away:

Missed Opportunities: Life presents countless opportunities for growth, success, and self-fulfillment. Failing to act on these opportunities can lead to a life filled with "what-ifs" and "could-have-beens."

Stagnation and Mediocrity: Those who resist growth often find themselves stuck in a cycle of mediocrity. Without progress, there is no improvement, and without improvement, one remains far from their full potential.

Regret and Frustration: The longer one delays pursuing their greatness, the greater the sense of regret. The realization that they had the chance to become something more but chose comfort over challenge can be painful.

Falling Behind in a Fast-Moving World: The world is constantly evolving. Those who fail to move forward will find themselves outpaced by those who embrace change, innovation, and continuous learning.

Loss of Purpose and Passion: When one does not actively pursue their greatness, life can feel empty. Passion fades,

"Decide today not to sit on your Greatness!"

motivation declines, and the drive to achieve something meaningful weakens.

How to Move in the Direction of Your Greatness

To ensure that greatness does not leave you behind, one must make a conscious effort to move forward. Here are steps to take:

Define Your Vision and Goals: Clearly articulate what greatness means to you. Set specific, achievable goals that align with your passions and purpose.

Take Action Consistently: Small steps toward your dreams are better than standing still. Progress, no matter how slow, keeps you moving in the right direction.

Embrace Challenges and Growth: Growth often comes from discomfort. Be willing to step out of your comfort zone and embrace challenges as opportunities to become stronger and wiser.

Stay Committed and Persistent: Greatness requires discipline and perseverance. There will be obstacles, but pushing through them will bring you closer to your potential.

"Decide today not to sit on your Greatness!"

Surround Yourself with Growth-Minded Individuals: The people around you influence your journey. Stay connected to those who encourage and inspire you to reach for more.

Learn and Evolve Constantly: Never stop learning. Whether through education, mentorship, or self-reflection, continuous improvement keeps you aligned with your greatness.

Take Risks and Trust the Process: Fear of failure can hold you back, but calculated risks often lead to the greatest rewards. Trust yourself and the process of growth.

Final Thoughts

Your greatness is a moving force—it does not wait, hesitate, or remain stagnant. It is up to you to chase after it, to walk boldly in its direction, and to take the necessary steps to make it a reality. If you do not, it will move forward without you, and you will be left wondering what could have been.

The choice is yours: either move toward your greatness or watch it leave you behind.

"Decide today not to sit on your Greatness!"

"Greatness Awaits You!
There Is Nothing Impossible For You"

"Decide today not to sit on your Greatness!"

"Greatness Awaits You!
There Is Nothing Impossible For You"

"Decide today not to sit on your Greatness!"

Chapter 18

It is important to keep moving forward towards the greatness in your future and not the failures of your past!

"Decide today not to sit on your Greatness!"

"Look to Jesus, the author and finisher of our faith."
Hebrew 12:2

Keep Moving Forward: Embracing Greatness and Leaving the Past Behind

Life is a journey filled with triumphs and setbacks, but what truly defines us is our ability to move forward. While the past holds valuable lessons, it should never become a prison that keeps us from stepping into our potential. It is essential to focus on the greatness that lies ahead rather than dwelling on past failures. Here's why embracing forward motion is crucial for personal growth, success, and fulfillment.

The Past Is a Teacher, Not a Destination

Failures and mistakes are part of the human experience. They provide lessons that shape our wisdom, resilience, and strength. However, the past should be seen as a classroom, not a home. If we fixate on past disappointments, we risk missing out on the opportunities and blessings awaiting us. Instead, we should extract the lessons and use them as stepping stones to propel us toward our future.

"Decide today not to sit on your Greatness!"

Growth Requires Movement

Every great achievement is built on progress. Stagnation is the enemy of success. When we continue moving forward—whether through learning, adapting, or evolving—we allow ourselves to grow into the person we are meant to be. Even in moments of uncertainty, taking small steps forward keeps us on the path to fulfillment.

Your Future Holds Greater Possibilities

The future is filled with endless opportunities, new experiences, and undiscovered potential. Holding on to past failures prevents us from embracing new possibilities. When we shift our focus toward what we can achieve rather than what we have lost, we cultivate a mindset of hope, ambition, and purpose.

Self-Forgiveness Is Key to Progress

Carrying the weight of past mistakes can hinder progress. Forgiving yourself is a powerful act that allows you to break free from regret and self-doubt. When you release past burdens, you create space for new beginnings and allow yourself to step boldly into your destiny.

"Decide today not to sit on your Greatness!"

The Best Version of You Is Ahead, Not Behind

Every day presents a new opportunity to improve, to be stronger, wiser, and more compassionate. The person you are becoming is far more significant than the person you used to be. By focusing on the greatness ahead, you set the stage for transformation and success.

Failure Is Not Final—It's Fuel

Many of the world's most successful individuals have faced significant setbacks. The difference between those who succeed and those who remain stuck in the past is resilience. Every failure carries a lesson that, when applied correctly, brings you closer to greatness. It is not the fall that defines you, but how you rise after it.

Your Purpose Demands Forward Motion

Each person has a unique purpose and calling in life. Dwelling on the past prevents us from fully stepping into that purpose. By choosing to move forward, we align ourselves with the destiny meant for us, unlocking our full potential.

"Decide today not to sit on your Greatness!"

Conclusion: Keep Moving Forward with Confidence

Life will always present challenges, but true greatness lies in the ability to keep pushing ahead despite obstacles. Let the past serve as a lesson, not a limitation. Your future is waiting for you—full of opportunities, growth, and success. Keep moving forward and embrace the greatness that is meant for you.

"Decide today not to sit on your Greatness!"

"Greatness Awaits You!
There Is Nothing Impossible For You"

"Decide today not to sit on your Greatness!"

"Greatness Awaits You!
There Is Nothing Impossible For You"

"Decide today not to sit on your Greatness!"

Chapter 19

"It is important to keep our eyes on the prize that is before us!"

"Decide today not to sit on your Greatness!"

Keeping Our Eyes on the Prize: The Power of Focus and Determination

Life is filled with distractions, obstacles, and challenges that can easily divert our attention from the goals and aspirations we set for ourselves. The phrase, **"Keep your eyes on the prize,"** is a powerful reminder of the importance of staying focused, determined, and unwavering in our pursuit of success. Whether in personal growth, career aspirations, or community efforts, maintaining our focus on the ultimate goal is essential to overcoming setbacks and achieving greatness.

Understanding the Prize

The "prize" represents our ultimate goal—whether it is a personal achievement, a career milestone, financial stability, educational attainment, or a transformative community initiative. It embodies the fulfillment of our dreams, the realization of our potential, and the positive impact we seek to make in our lives and the lives of others. However, achieving the prize requires discipline, persistence, and the ability to remain steadfast despite inevitable obstacles.

"Decide today not to sit on your Greatness!"

Challenges That Test Our Focus

Distractions and Temptations

In a world filled with social media, entertainment, and countless demands on our time, it is easy to lose focus on what truly matters. Distractions can lead us to procrastinate, make unwise decisions, or stray from our goals.

Fear and Self-Doubt

Many people abandon their dreams due to a fear of failure or feelings of inadequacy. Doubt can make us second-guess our capabilities and deter us from taking bold steps toward our goals.

Unexpected Setbacks

Challenges such as financial difficulties, health issues, or personal losses can make achieving our goals seem impossible. These obstacles test our resilience and commitment.

Negative Influences

The people around us can either lift us up or pull us down. Negative influences, discouragement, and toxic environments can make it harder to stay committed to our vision.

"Decide today not to sit on your Greatness!"

The Power of Staying Focused

Clarity of Purpose

Clearly defining our goals helps us stay on track. Writing down specific objectives and breaking them into smaller steps makes the journey more manageable and measurable.

Developing a Strong Mindset

Success is largely dependent on our mindset. A growth-oriented mindset allows us to embrace challenges as learning opportunities rather than setbacks.

Surrounding Ourselves with the Right People

Being around individuals who uplift, encourage, and challenge us to be better helps reinforce our commitment to the prize.

Daily Reminders and Affirmations

Regularly visualizing the end goal and affirming our ability to achieve it keeps motivation high. Creating vision boards, journaling progress, and celebrating small wins help maintain enthusiasm.

"Decide today not to sit on your Greatness!"

Resilience and Adaptability

No journey is without difficulties, but resilience allows us to bounce back from failures and keep moving forward. Being flexible in our approach while staying committed to the goal is key.

Taking Action Consistently

Small, consistent steps lead to significant achievements. Progress is made not through occasional bursts of effort but through sustained and disciplined actions over time.

Examples of Staying Focused on the Prize

Historical Figures

Civil rights leaders like Dr. Martin Luther King Jr. and Nelson Mandela remained focused on their visions for justice and equality despite opposition, setbacks, and hardships.

Athletes and Entrepreneurs

Successful athletes like Serena Williams or business leaders like Oprah Winfrey overcame obstacles by maintaining their focus, pushing through difficulties, and staying committed to their dreams.

"Decide today not to sit on your Greatness!"

Personal Success Stories

Many people have risen from poverty, difficult childhoods, or personal tragedies by keeping their eyes on their goals and refusing to give up.

Conclusion

Keeping our eyes on the prize is essential for success in any endeavor. Challenges will arise, distractions will come, and moments of doubt may shake our confidence. However, by staying focused, developing resilience, and maintaining a strong sense of purpose, we can push through any adversity and achieve the greatness that lies ahead. The key to success is not just dreaming but remaining dedicated to the journey until the prize is within reach.

"Decide today not to sit on your Greatness!"

"Greatness Awaits You!
There Is Nothing Impossible For You"

"Decide today not to sit on your Greatness!"

"Greatness Awaits You!
There Is Nothing Impossible For You"

"Decide today not to sit on your Greatness!"

Chapter 20

"Know this you are destined for greatness."

"Decide today not to sit on your Greatness!"

"Greatness Awaits You!
There Is Nothing Impossible For You"

Introduction

"Know This: You Are Destined for Greatness" is more than just a phrase; it is a declaration of purpose, a call to action, and a mindset that inspires individuals to recognize their potential and strive for excellence. It is a philosophy that reminds us that each person is born with unique talents, abilities, and a divine purpose that, when embraced, leads to a life of fulfillment and impact.

The Meaning Behind the Statement

"Know This" – The Power of Awareness

The phrase begins with a command to "Know This," emphasizing certainty and awareness. It challenges individuals to shift their mindset from self-doubt to confidence.

Many people live without realizing their own greatness, often trapped in cycles of fear, insecurity, or external limitations. The first step to achieving anything remarkable is acknowledging that greatness is not reserved for a select few—it is within everyone.

Awareness breeds action. When you truly "know" something, you begin to act on it, believe in it, and align your life choices with that truth.

"Decide today not to sit on your Greatness!"

"Greatness Awaits You!
There Is Nothing Impossible For You"

"You Are Destined" – The Certainty of Purpose

This part of the statement reinforces that greatness is not accidental or conditional; it is something planned and set in motion.

Destiny implies a higher calling—a preordained path that leads to significant achievements and contributions to the world.

While destiny exists, it requires effort, discipline, and perseverance to bring it to fruition. Knowing you are destined for greatness should serve as motivation to pursue excellence, even in the face of adversity.

"For Greatness" – The Ultimate Aspiration

Greatness is not just about personal success; it is about leaving a lasting impact on others, inspiring change, and maximizing one's potential.

It manifests in various ways—through leadership, service, creativity, innovation, and resilience.

Greatness is not about perfection but about striving to be the best version of oneself, constantly growing, learning, and evolving.

"Decide today not to sit on your Greatness!"

"Greatness Awaits You!
There Is Nothing Impossible For You"

The Mindset of Greatness:

Living by the principle of "Know This: You Are Destined for Greatness" requires cultivating a mindset of growth and excellence. Here are key principles to embody this mindset:

Self-Belief – Trust in your abilities and recognize that you have what it takes to succeed.

Purpose-Driven Living – Align your actions with your greater purpose and values.

Resilience – Overcome setbacks with determination, knowing that challenges are stepping stones to success.

Continuous Learning – Invest in personal and professional development to refine your skills and knowledge.

Service to Others – True greatness is measured not just by what you achieve but by how you uplift others.

Boldness and Courage – Take risks, step outside of your comfort zone, and pursue your dreams with confidence.

"Decide today not to sit on your Greatness!"

Conclusion:

"Know This: You Are Destined for Greatness" is a powerful affirmation that challenges individuals to see themselves through the lens of potential and purpose. It serves as a reminder that each person has the ability to rise above limitations, influence the world positively, and leave a legacy of impact. By embracing this truth, one can unlock the doors to success, fulfillment, and a life of meaning.

"Decide today not to sit on your Greatness!"

"Greatness Awaits You!
There Is Nothing Impossible For You"

"Decide today not to sit on your Greatness!"

"Greatness Awaits You!
There Is Nothing Impossible For You"

"Decide today not to sit on your Greatness!"

Chapter 21

Make sure you are always walking in your greatness no matter what life throws your way!

"Decide today not to sit on your Greatness!"

Walking in Your Greatness: No Matter What Life Throws Your Way

Life is an unpredictable journey, full of highs and lows, triumphs and setbacks. Every individual will face challenges—some expected, others completely unforeseen. However, what defines a person is not the obstacles they encounter, but how they respond to them. Walking in your greatness means consistently striving to be your best self, regardless of the difficulties you may face. It requires confidence, resilience, and an unshakable belief in your purpose. Here's how to ensure that you are always walking in your greatness, no matter what life throws your way.

1. **Understand and Own Your Greatness**

The first step to walking in your greatness is recognizing that you are inherently valuable and capable. Your greatness is not based on external achievements but on the unique gifts, strengths, and qualities you bring to the world. It is rooted in your purpose, passion, and the impact you have on others.

Acknowledge Your Strengths – Make a list of your skills, talents, and accomplishments to remind yourself of how much you have already overcome.

"Decide today not to sit on your Greatness!"

Embrace Your Uniqueness – There is no one else like you. Your journey, experiences, and perspective are distinct and valuable.

Affirm Your Worth – Speak positivity over your life. Use affirmations such as "I am powerful," "I am worthy," and "I am walking in my greatness every day."

2. **Develop a Resilient Mindset**

Greatness is not about never falling—it's about always getting back up. Resilience is the ability to bounce back from adversity with strength and wisdom.

Shift Your Perspective on Challenges – Instead of seeing obstacles as roadblocks, view them as opportunities for growth. Every setback teaches a lesson that can propel you forward.

Stay Solution-Oriented – When faced with difficulties, focus on finding solutions instead of dwelling on problems.

Practice Gratitude – Gratitude shifts your mindset from lack to abundance. Even in tough times, find something to be thankful for.

3. **Maintain Your Integrity and Character**

"Decide today not to sit on your Greatness!"

"Greatness Awaits You!
There Is Nothing Impossible For You"

True greatness is not just about personal success; it is also about the way you treat others and the values you uphold.

Live with Integrity – Stay true to your principles, even when it is difficult. Doing what is right will always lead to long-term success.

Lead with Kindness and Compassion – Lift others as you rise. Encourage, support, and inspire those around you.

Stay Humble and Teachable – No matter how much success you achieve, there is always room for growth. Keep learning, evolving, and improving.

4.   Keep Moving Forward, No Matter What

Life will throw obstacles in your way—disappointments, failures, and unexpected hardships. The key to greatness is persistence.

Set Goals and Stay Focused – Clearly define what you want to achieve and take steps every day to move closer to your goals.

Adapt and Overcome – Be flexible and willing to adjust when necessary. Sometimes the path to success is not a straight line.

"Decide today not to sit on your Greatness!"

Never Give Up on Yourself – Even when things seem impossible, remember that you have the strength to push through. You are more capable than you think.

5. Surround Yourself with Positive Influences

The people around you can either propel you forward or hold you back. Choose wisely.

Build a Supportive Network – Surround yourself with people who inspire, encourage, and challenge you to be better.

Distance Yourself from Negativity – Avoid toxic relationships, negative self-talk, and environments that diminish your greatness.

Seek Mentorship and Guidance – Learning from those who have already walked the path of greatness can help you navigate your journey more effectively.

6. Stay True to Your Purpose

Greatness is not just about personal gain; it is about fulfilling your purpose and making an impact.

"Decide today not to sit on your Greatness!"

Identify Your Purpose – What drives you? What brings you joy and fulfillment? Align your actions with your deeper purpose.

Serve Others – Use your gifts and talents to uplift those around you. True greatness is found in giving and making a difference.

Stay Consistent – Your purpose is a lifelong journey. Stay committed, even when progress seems slow.

Final Thoughts

Walking in your greatness is a daily choice. It is about showing up as your best self, even when life gets tough. It means believing in yourself, overcoming obstacles with resilience, staying true to your values, and pursuing your purpose with passion. No matter what life throws your way, remember: you were born for greatness. Keep walking boldly in it.

"Decide today not to sit on your Greatness!"

"Greatness Awaits You!
There Is Nothing Impossible For You"

"Decide today not to sit on your Greatness!"

"Greatness Awaits You!
There Is Nothing Impossible For You"

"Decide today not to sit on your Greatness!"

Chapter 22

"This is the mighty power that God has for you!"

"Decide today not to sit on your Greatness!"

"Greatness Awaits You!
There Is Nothing Impossible For You"

In the book of Ephesians 1:19 God says, "I pray that you will continually experience the immeasurable greatness of God's power made available to you through faith. Then your lives will be an advertisement of this immense power as it works through you!

In the journey of faith and purpose, we often encounter moments of doubt, fear, and uncertainty. However, there is a mighty power that God has for you—one that transforms, uplifts, and strengthens you beyond your own limitations. This divine power is not just an abstract concept but a tangible force that can reshape your life, unlock your potential, and lead you to victory in every aspect of your journey.

1. **The Power of Unshakable Faith**

God grants you the power to believe even when circumstances seem impossible. Faith moves mountains, breaks chains, and opens doors that no man can shut. When you trust in God's promises, you activate His supernatural power in your life. His power allows you to see beyond the present struggles and into the victorious future He has prepared for you.

"Decide today not to sit on your Greatness!"

2. **The Power of Transformation**

God's power is not just about external blessings—it is also about an internal renewal. The moment you allow Him to work in your life, He transforms your heart, mind, and spirit. You are no longer bound by your past mistakes, pain, or failures. Instead, you become a new creation, filled with wisdom, purpose, and divine strength.

3. **The Power of Strength in Weakness**

One of the greatest demonstrations of God's power is how He gives strength in times of weakness. When you feel like you can't go on, He lifts you up. When life's burdens become too heavy, He carries you. His grace is sufficient, and His power is made perfect in your weakness. Through Him, you can overcome every obstacle, defeat every enemy, and rise stronger than before.

4. **The Power of Miracles and Breakthroughs**

God is still in the business of miracles. His power can turn impossibilities into testimonies. Whether you need healing, deliverance, financial breakthrough, or restoration in relationships, God's mighty power is available to move in your life. He is the same God who parted the Red Sea, made the blind see, and raised the dead—His power has not changed!

"Decide today not to sit on your Greatness!"

5. The Power of Purpose and Calling

God's power is not just about survival; it's about thriving in the purpose He created you for. He has equipped you with gifts, talents, and a calling that no one else can fulfill. When you surrender to Him, He aligns your steps with divine purpose, opening doors of opportunity and positioning you for greatness.

6. The Power of Divine Protection

God's power serves as a shield around you. No weapon formed against you shall prosper. His angels are commanded to guard you in all your ways. Whether in times of spiritual warfare or physical danger, His power ensures that you remain under His divine covering.

7. The Power of Everlasting Love

Above all, God's power is rooted in His unfailing love for you. His love never wavers, never fails, and never gives up on you. No matter where you've been or what you've done, His power of redemption is always available. You are His beloved child, and nothing can separate you from His love.

"Decide today not to sit on your Greatness!"

Activate This Power in Your Life!

To fully experience this mighty power, you must:

- ✓ Seek Him through prayer and devotion.
- ✓ Strengthen your faith by standing on His promises.
- ✓ Walk in obedience and trust His plan for your life.
- ✓ Allow the Holy Spirit to guide and empower you daily.

God has given you mighty power—not just for yourself, but to be a light in the world. Walk boldly in His power and watch as He does exceedingly and abundantly beyond all that you could ask or imagine! 🔥✨

"For God has not given us a spirit of fear, but of power, love, and a sound mind." — 2 Timothy 1:7

"Know This Your Faith Is Bigger Than Your Fear!"

"Decide today not to sit on your Greatness!"

"Greatness Awaits You!
There Is Nothing Impossible For You"

"Decide today not to sit on your Greatness!"

"Greatness Awaits You!
There Is Nothing Impossible For You"

"Decide today not to sit on your Greatness!"

Chapter 23

We must keep moving forward in the direction God is sending us. Because He has new doors, He wants to open for us!

"Decide today not to sit on your Greatness!"

Moving Forward in the Direction God is Sending Us

Life is a journey filled with seasons of challenges, growth, and transformation. As believers, we are called to move forward, trusting that God is guiding our steps toward His divine purpose. No matter the obstacles we face or the uncertainty that lies ahead, our faith compels us to keep pressing on, knowing that God is leading us toward something greater.

God does not intend for us to remain stagnant or trapped in the past. He desires for us to embrace change, step out in faith, and walk boldly toward the future He has prepared for us. When we follow His direction, we align ourselves with His perfect will, positioning ourselves for new blessings, opportunities, and breakthroughs.

Trusting God's Plan

Sometimes, moving forward means leaving behind familiar places, relationships, or mindsets that no longer serve God's purpose for our lives. It can be difficult to let go of the past, especially when it feels comfortable or safe. However, we must remember that God's plans are always greater than our own. When He closes one door, it is because He has something better in store.

"Decide today not to sit on your Greatness!"

"Greatness Awaits You!
There Is Nothing Impossible For You"

Proverbs 3:5-6 reminds us:
"Trust in the Lord with all your heart and lean not on your own understanding; in all your ways submit to Him, and He will make your paths straight."

God's direction may not always make sense to us in the moment, but He sees the full picture. Our responsibility is to trust Him, obey His calling, and move forward with confidence, knowing that He is orchestrating every step for our good.

Overcoming Fear and Doubt

Fear and doubt often try to hold us back from moving forward. The enemy wants us to remain stuck in worry, discouragement, or complacency. But God calls us to walk in faith, not fear. Isaiah 41:10 reminds us:

"So do not fear, for I am with you; do not be dismayed, for I am your God. I will strengthen you and help you; I will uphold you with my righteous right hand."

When we trust in God's promises, we gain the strength and courage to step into the unknown, knowing that He is with us. We do not have to be afraid of what is ahead because the One who goes before us is faithful.

"Decide today not to sit on your Greatness!"

God's New Doors of Opportunity

God is always working behind the scenes, preparing new doors of opportunity, favor, and provision. He desires to take us to new levels of spiritual growth, purpose, and impact. But in order to experience these new blessings, we must be willing to walk through the doors He opens.

Revelation 3:8 says:
"See, I have placed before you an open door that no one can shut."

When God opens a door, no force in this world can close it. However, we must be ready to step forward in obedience. Delays and distractions can cause us to miss what God has prepared, but when we move in faith, we will see His promises come to pass.

Moving Forward with Purpose

Each day is an opportunity to grow, to learn, and to step deeper into God's calling for our lives. Moving forward does not mean rushing ahead on our own but rather walking in alignment with His guidance. It means seeking Him daily in prayer, staying rooted in His Word, and being sensitive to the leading of the Holy Spirit.

If God is calling you to something greater—whether it's a new job, ministry, relationship, or spiritual breakthrough—

"Decide today not to sit on your Greatness!"

do not hesitate. Take the next step with boldness, knowing that He is paving the way.

Conclusion

God's plans for us are filled with hope, purpose, and abundance. When we surrender to His direction and keep moving forward, we will witness His power at work in our lives. No matter what you are facing today, remember that God has new doors waiting to be opened for you. Keep trusting, keep believing, and keep walking forward in faith—because His best is yet to come!

"Decide today not to sit on your Greatness!"

"Greatness Awaits You!
There Is Nothing Impossible For You"

"Decide today not to sit on your Greatness!"

"Greatness Awaits You!
There Is Nothing Impossible For You"

"Decide today not to sit on your Greatness!"

Chapter 24

What Good Is Living a Life You've Been Gifted If You Are Not Using the Gifts of Greatness, You Have Been Given?

"Decide today not to sit on your Greatness!"

"Greatness Awaits You!
There Is Nothing Impossible For You"

Life is a precious and extraordinary gift, filled with opportunities, experiences, and the ability to contribute meaningfully to the world. Each person is born with unique talents, skills, and capabilities that set them apart, designed to not only bring personal fulfillment but also to serve others and make an impact. However, many people go through life unaware of or unwilling to fully utilize these gifts, settling for mediocrity or conforming to societal expectations rather than stepping into their full potential.

The question, *"What good is living a life you've been gifted if you are not using the gifts of greatness, you have been given?"* is a call to action. It challenges individuals to reflect on whether they are truly maximizing their potential and making the most of the abilities they have been blessed with. Below, we explore the deeper meaning behind this question and why it is essential to use one's gifts of greatness.

Understanding the Concept of Gifts and Greatness

Every individual possesses intrinsic gifts—natural talents, passions, and skills that, when developed, can lead to excellence and fulfillment. These gifts can manifest in various forms, such as creativity, leadership, problem-solving, empathy, resilience, and innovation. Some people are born with the ability to inspire others, while others have analytical minds capable of solving complex problems.

"Decide today not to sit on your Greatness!"

Some may have artistic talents, while others possess entrepreneurial spirits.

Greatness is not solely about fame, wealth, or power; it is about realizing and maximizing one's potential in a way that positively impacts the world. True greatness is about self-mastery, continuous growth, and serving others. It is about pushing past fear, doubt, and complacency to become the best version of oneself.

The Consequences of Neglecting One's Gifts

Failing to use one's gifts results in a life of unfulfilled potential. When people ignore their talents or refuse to develop them, they experience a variety of consequences, including:

A. Regret and Unfulfillment

Many people reach the later stages of life realizing they never pursued their dreams or utilized their talents to the fullest. Regret often stems not from failure but from never having tried in the first place. Living a life without exploring one's full potential leads to an underlying sense of dissatisfaction.

B. A Life of Mediocrity

When people choose comfort over growth, they remain stuck in mediocrity. They settle for jobs that don't chal-

"Decide today not to sit on your Greatness!"

lenge them, relationships that don't inspire them, and routines that don't excite them. Mediocrity is the enemy of greatness, as it prevents people from experiencing the richness that life has to offer.

C. A Missed Opportunity to Make an Impact

Each person's gifts are not meant only for themselves; they are meant to serve others as well. The world needs what each individual has to offer. Whether it's a brilliant idea, a song that can heal hearts, an invention that can change lives, or simply the ability to encourage others, not using one's gifts means withholding something valuable from the world.

D. Emotional and Spiritual Stagnation

Neglecting one's gifts often leads to feelings of frustration, restlessness, or even depression. A person who is not growing or evolving in alignment with their purpose feels disconnected from their true self. Using one's talents provides a sense of purpose and fulfillment, which leads to greater happiness and well-being.

The Power of Using One's Gifts

When individuals embrace and develop their gifts, they experience life on a different level. They unlock doors of

"Decide today not to sit on your Greatness!"

opportunity, create meaningful experiences, and contribute to the greater good. Here's how using one's gifts leads to a life of significance:

Personal Fulfillment and Joy

There is no greater satisfaction than knowing you are living in alignment with your true potential. When people use their gifts, they feel more alive, purposeful, and driven. Engaging in activities that utilize their natural abilities brings joy and a deep sense of accomplishment.

Inspiring and Uplifting Others

Greatness is contagious. When one person steps into their full potential, they inspire those around them to do the same. Whether through mentorship, leadership, or creative expression, using one's gifts has a ripple effect, encouraging others to explore their own talents.

Creating a Lasting Legacy

People who maximize their gifts leave behind a legacy that extends beyond their lifetime. Whether through groundbreaking inventions, impactful leadership, or community transformation, those who use their talents effectively make an indelible mark on the world. Their contributions continue to inspire generations.

"Decide today not to sit on your Greatness!"

"Greatness Awaits You!
There Is Nothing Impossible For You"

Elevating Society as a Whole

When individuals rise to their full potential, society benefits. Innovation flourishes, solutions to global challenges emerge, and new ideas reshape industries. The world advances because individuals choose to harness their abilities and contribute to progress.

Steps to Unlock and Use Your Gifts

If you feel you are not fully utilizing your talents, here are some steps to help you step into your greatness:

Self-Discovery

Reflect on what you are naturally good at.

Identify activities that bring you joy and make you lose track of time.

Seek feedback from trusted mentors, friends, or family who recognize your strengths.

Invest in Growth

Take courses, attend workshops, or seek mentorship in areas where you have potential.

"Decide today not to sit on your Greatness!"

"Greatness Awaits You!
There Is Nothing Impossible For You"

Read books and continuously educate yourself to sharpen your skills.

Practice and refine your talents regularly.

Overcome Fear and Doubt

Recognize that fear is a normal part of growth, but don't let it paralyze you.

Replace negative self-talk with affirmations and confidence-building habits.

Take small steps toward your goals and gradually expand your comfort zone.

Share Your Gifts

Find ways to contribute your talents to your community or workplace.

Volunteer, mentor, or teach others what you know.

Use social media, blogs, or public speaking to share your knowledge and inspire others.

"Decide today not to sit on your Greatness!"

Stay Consistent and Committed

Greatness is not achieved overnight; it requires dedication and perseverance.

Set clear goals and develop habits that align with your strengths.

Stay connected with like-minded individuals who encourage and challenge you.

Conclusion: A Call to Live a Life of Purpose

Life is too short and too valuable to be lived passively. Each person has been gifted with talents and abilities that are meant to be nurtured, developed, and shared with the world. Choosing to step into one's greatness is a conscious decision—one that requires courage, dedication, and the willingness to go beyond comfort and mediocrity.

The question *"What good is living a life you've been gifted if you are not using the gifts of greatness, you have been given?"* is an invitation to wake up to your full potential. It is a reminder that you were created with a purpose and that your talents are not just for your own benefit but for the enrichment of others as well.

"Decide today not to sit on your Greatness!"

"Greatness Awaits You!
There Is Nothing Impossible For You"

If you are not already using your gifts to their fullest extent, now is the time to start. Take ownership of your strengths, embrace challenges, and commit to living a life that reflects your highest capabilities. The world needs your greatness—don't let it go to waste.

"Decide today not to sit on your Greatness!"

"Greatness Awaits You!
There Is Nothing Impossible For You"

"Decide today not to sit on your Greatness!"

"Greatness Awaits You!
There Is Nothing Impossible For You"

"Decide today not to sit on your Greatness!"

Chapter 25

When you are moving forward toward your greatness, it is a clear indication that you are making things happen in your life.

"Decide today not to sit on your Greatness!"

"Greatness Awaits You!
There Is Nothing Impossible For You"

Greatness is not an accident, nor is it something that happens overnight. It is a journey, a continuous process of growth, self-improvement, and action. When you are moving forward toward your greatness, it is a clear indication that you are making things happen in your life. This movement signifies progress, determination, and a commitment to becoming the best version of yourself.

Understanding the Journey to Greatness:

Greatness is not defined by perfection but by persistence. It is the ability to rise after a fall, to keep pushing despite challenges, and to embrace the lessons that come with every step of the journey. It is about setting meaningful goals, aligning your actions with your purpose, and continuously striving to achieve new heights.

When you are on the path to greatness, you experience growth in multiple areas of your life—mentally, emotionally, physically, and spiritually. This transformation is visible in the way you think, the way you act, and the way you influence those around you.

Signs That You Are Moving Towards Your Greatness:

One of the biggest indicators that you are making things happen in your life is that you are no longer just dreaming

"Decide today not to sit on your Greatness!"

about success—you are actively working toward it. You are setting goals, making plans, and executing them with dedication. Dreamers imagine what is possible, but doers take action to turn their dreams into reality.

You Are Overcoming Fear and Self-Doubt:

Fear and self-doubt are natural emotions, but when you are truly moving towards greatness, you refuse to let them hold you back. Instead of allowing fear to paralyze you, you push forward with courage, knowing that growth happens outside of your comfort zone.

You Are Learning From Failures and Mistakes:

A person committed to their greatness does not see failure as the end but as an opportunity to learn and grow. Every setback becomes a stepping stone, every mistake a lesson, and every challenge a chance to become stronger. If you are using your experiences to improve rather than to quit, you are making progress.

You Are Consistently Improving Yourself:

Growth is continuous. When you are on the path to greatness, you are constantly seeking ways to improve your skills, knowledge, and mindset. Whether through educa-

"Decide today not to sit on your Greatness!"

tion, mentorship, training, or self-reflection, you are always evolving into a better version of yourself.

You Are Surrounded by Growth-Oriented People:

The company you keep reflects your journey. If you find yourself surrounded by motivated, forward-thinking, and ambitious individuals, it is a sign that you are aligning yourself with success. Greatness attracts greatness, and being in the right environment encourages further growth.

You Are Helping Others Along the Way:

True greatness is not just about personal success—it is also about lifting others up. When you start using your knowledge, experience, and success to inspire and support others, you are making a significant impact. Helping others is a reflection of true leadership and purpose-driven success.

You Feel a Sense of Purpose and Fulfillment:

When you are moving toward greatness, your life feels purposeful. You wake up with excitement, eager to tackle the day's challenges. Your actions are aligned with your passions, and the work you do brings a sense of fulfillment and joy.

"Decide today not to sit on your Greatness!"

The Power of Persistence and Belief:

The road to greatness is not always easy. It requires persistence, resilience, and an unwavering belief in yourself. There will be times of doubt, obstacles to overcome, and moments when giving up seems like an option. But if you keep moving forward—no matter how slow—progress is being made.

Remember, the fact that you are striving for something greater means you are already ahead of those who choose to remain stagnant. Every step you take towards your dreams, every effort you make to improve, and every lesson you learn is a testament that you are making things happen in your life.

Conclusion:

Moving forward toward your greatness is a sign that you are taking control of your destiny. It shows that you refuse to settle, that you are willing to do the work, and that you are committed to achieving something meaningful. Keep pushing, keep growing, and keep believing in yourself— because as long as you are moving forward, you are making things happen in your life!

"Decide today not to sit on your Greatness!"

"Greatness Awaits You!
There Is Nothing Impossible For You"

"Decide today not to sit on your Greatness!"

"Greatness Awaits You!
There Is Nothing Impossible For You"

"Decide today not to sit on your Greatness!"

Chapter 26

"Whenever you find yourself doubting whether or not you can make it, just remember how far you have come and the battles you have already won!"

"Decide today not to sit on your Greatness!"

"Greatness Awaits You!
There Is Nothing Impossible For You"

Life's journey is filled with challenges, uncertainties, and moments of doubt. At times, you may find yourself questioning whether you have the strength to continue, whether you are truly capable of achieving your goals, or whether your struggles will ever lead to success. However, in those moments of self-doubt, it is essential to pause and reflect on just how far you have come.

Acknowledge Your Progress

Every step you have taken, no matter how small, has brought you closer to your dreams. You have endured setbacks, faced adversity, and yet, you are still here standing, striving, and pushing forward. The journey you have traveled is proof of your resilience. The fact that you are contemplating your next move, despite the doubts, is evidence of your determination.

Recognize the Battles You Have Already Won

Think about the moments when you felt like giving up but didn't. The battles you fought—whether internal struggles with self-doubt, external challenges in your career, relationships, or personal growth—have shaped you into the person you are today. You have conquered obstacles you once thought were insurmountable. You have healed from pains that once seemed unbearable. These victories, whether big

"Decide today not to sit on your Greatness!"

or small, are reminders that you have the strength to overcome whatever lies ahead.

The Power of Resilience

Resilience is not just about bouncing back—it is about moving forward with newfound wisdom and strength. When you reflect on your past struggles, you realize that you are far more capable than your doubts suggest. Every hardship you have faced has equipped you with the tools to navigate future challenges. You have grown through your experiences, learned valuable lessons, and developed a perseverance that will carry you through the next phase of your journey.

The Journey is Proof That You Can Succeed

If you ever find yourself wondering if you can make it, remember that you have already made it through so much. The person you were in the past may not have believed they could reach where you are today, yet here you stand. This alone is proof that you are stronger than you think. Trust in your journey, believe in your abilities, and remind yourself that success is not just about the destination—it is about the courage to keep going.

"Decide today not to sit on your Greatness!"

A Future Built on Strength

As you move forward, carry this mindset with you: Your past victories are a testament to your future success. The challenges you face today will soon become the victories you reflect on tomorrow. Stay committed, stay focused, and remember—whenever doubt creeps in, let your past achievements remind you of the warrior within.

Conclusion:

Whenever you find yourself doubting whether or not you can make it, just remember how far you have come and the battles you have already won. You are capable, you are strong, and you are destined for greatness. Keep pushing forward!

"Decide today not to sit on your Greatness!"

"Greatness Awaits You!
There Is Nothing Impossible For You"

"Decide today not to sit on your Greatness!"

"Greatness Awaits You!
There Is Nothing Impossible For You"

"Decide today not to sit on your Greatness!"

Chapter 27

"When you have made peace with your past, you can move forward to the greatness in your future!"

"Decide today not to sit on your Greatness!"

"Greatness Awaits You!
There Is Nothing Impossible For You"

Life is a journey filled with experiences—some joyful, some painful, and others that leave lasting imprints on our hearts and minds. The past, with all its triumphs and trials, plays a significant role in shaping who we are today. However, holding onto the pain, regrets, and disappointments of the past can act as chains that keep us from stepping into the fullness of our future.

Making peace with the past is a transformative process that involves self-reflection, acceptance, forgiveness, and personal growth. It is not about erasing memories or denying what has happened but rather about acknowledging those experiences, learning from them, and choosing not to let them define your future. When you come to terms with your past, you free yourself from its grip, allowing yourself to embrace new opportunities and walk boldly into your destiny.

The Power of Acceptance

Acceptance is the first step in making peace with your past. It requires recognizing that the events of yesterday cannot be changed but can serve as lessons for tomorrow. Whether it's mistakes you've made, hurts you've endured, or setbacks you've encountered, accepting them means you no longer resist or live in denial. Instead, you acknowledge what has happened and use it as a foundation for personal growth.

"Decide today not to sit on your Greatness!"

The Role of Forgiveness

Forgiveness is one of the most powerful tools in achieving peace. This includes forgiving yourself for past decisions and mistakes, as well as forgiving those who may have wronged you. Holding onto resentment and bitterness only burdens your spirit, keeping you emotionally tied to negative experiences. When you release these emotions, you create space for healing and renewal.

Forgiving does not mean condoning hurtful actions or forgetting the lessons learned. It means choosing to free yourself from the emotional baggage that weighs you down. It is an act of self-liberation, allowing you to move forward with clarity, strength, and purpose.

Breaking Free from the Past's Control

Many people allow their past failures, heartbreaks, and disappointments to dictate their future. They remain stuck in patterns of self-doubt, fear, or unworthiness. However, once you make peace with your past, you reclaim control over your narrative. You begin to realize that your past does not define you—your choices today do.

Breaking free involves shifting your mindset from victimhood to empowerment. It means taking responsibility for your present and future, regardless of what has happened

"Decide today not to sit on your Greatness!"

before. You stop allowing past circumstances to determine your worth or limit your potential. Instead, you use those experiences as stepping stones toward a greater future.

Embracing Growth and Change

Growth comes when you allow yourself to change. Once you have made peace with your past, you are no longer bound by old limitations. You start seeing opportunities where you once saw obstacles. You take risks with confidence, knowing that your past has equipped you with wisdom and resilience.

Every great future requires a willingness to evolve. When you let go of old wounds, you make room for new blessings. When you release past regrets, you create space for new achievements. Your greatness lies not in what has happened to you, but in how you rise above it.

Stepping into Your Greatness

Your future holds infinite possibilities. Once you have healed from the past, you are free to embrace the greatness that awaits you. This could mean stepping into your purpose, pursuing new dreams, cultivating meaningful relationships, or simply living with more peace and joy.

"Decide today not to sit on your Greatness!"

"Greatness Awaits You!
There Is Nothing Impossible For You"

Greatness is not just about success in the external world—it's about internal fulfillment. It's about becoming the best version of yourself, unburdened by past pain, and fully embracing the life you were meant to live.

Conclusion

Making peace with your past is one of the most liberating things you can do for yourself. It allows you to move forward without the weight of yesterday holding you back. By accepting, forgiving, and growing from your experiences, you unlock the door to a future filled with purpose, joy, and boundless possibilities.

When you have made peace with your past, you step into a future where greatness is not just a possibility—it's your destiny!

"Decide today not to sit on your Greatness!"

"Greatness Awaits You!
There Is Nothing Impossible For You"

"Decide today not to sit on your Greatness!"

"Greatness Awaits You!
There Is Nothing Impossible For You"

"Decide today not to sit on your Greatness!"

Chapter 28

"You must own all of your greatness."

Lisa Nichols

"Decide today not to sit on your Greatness!"

"Greatness Awaits You!
There Is Nothing Impossible For You"

You Must Own All of Your Greatness

Greatness is not something given; it is something cultivated, developed, and ultimately embraced. Many people spend their lives waiting for external validation to confirm their worth, but true power comes from within. To fully step into the highest version of yourself, you must own all of your greatness—your strengths, your wisdom, your accomplishments, and even your struggles.

Understanding Your Greatness

Greatness is not just about achievements or public recognition; it is about the totality of who you are. It includes:

Your Strengths: The natural talents and skills you possess that make you uniquely powerful.

Your Experiences: Every lesson learned, every hardship overcome, and every milestone reached.

Your Character: The values, principles, and integrity that shape how you move through life.

Your Resilience: The ability to rise above difficulties, adapt, and continue to grow.

"Decide today not to sit on your Greatness!"

Owning your greatness means acknowledging all aspects of your journey—both the wins and the challenges. It requires confidence, self-awareness, and the courage to stand in your truth without apology.

Why People Struggle to Own Their Greatness

Many individuals have difficulty accepting their own greatness due to various internal and external factors:

Self-Doubt: The fear of not being "enough" can cause people to shrink instead of stepping into their full potential.

Imposter Syndrome: Even the most accomplished individuals sometimes feel like they don't deserve success.

Societal Conditioning: Society often encourages humility to the point where people feel guilty for embracing their strengths.

Comparison Culture: Constantly measuring yourself against others can make you feel inadequate instead of appreciating your own unique gifts.

Breaking free from these limitations requires a mindset shift—one that prioritizes self-recognition, affirmation,

"Decide today not to sit on your Greatness!"

and the belief that you are worthy of every success you achieve.

How to Fully Own Your Greatness

Acknowledge Your Journey

Reflect on your past struggles and triumphs. Every challenge you have faced has contributed to the person you are today.

Make a list of your accomplishments—big and small—to remind yourself of how far you have come.

Speak Positively About Yourself

Replace self-criticism with self-affirmation. Instead of saying, "I'm not good enough," declare, "I am constantly growing and evolving."

Surround yourself with people who recognize and celebrate your greatness.

Embrace Your Unique Gifts

Stop comparing yourself to others and recognize that your journey is uniquely yours.

"Decide today not to sit on your Greatness!"

"Greatness Awaits You!
There Is Nothing Impossible For You"

Invest in developing your talents and skills further so you can maximize your potential.

Step Into Leadership

Lead with confidence, whether in your community, workplace, or personal life.

Use your greatness to inspire and uplift others.

Own Your Flaws and Learn from Them

True greatness is not about being perfect but about continuously learning and improving.

Accept mistakes as stepping stones to growth rather than signs of failure.

Celebrate Yourself

Do not downplay your achievements. Give yourself credit where credit is due.

Make self-care and self-recognition a priority.

"Decide today not to sit on your Greatness!"

The Impact of Owning Your Greatness

When you fully own your greatness, you become unstoppable. You exude confidence, attract opportunities, and inspire those around you. More importantly, you set a precedent for others to embrace their own potential.

By stepping boldly into your greatness, you become a beacon of light for those still searching for theirs. Your courage gives others permission to rise, and your presence in the world becomes a testament to the power of self-belief.

So, stand tall, claim your space, and own all of your greatness—because the world needs you at your fullest potential.

"Decide today not to sit on your Greatness!"

"Greatness Awaits You!
There Is Nothing Impossible For You"

"Decide today not to sit on your Greatness!"

"Greatness Awaits You!
There Is Nothing Impossible For You"

"Decide today not to sit on your Greatness!"